Citrus

How to Grow and Use Citrus Fruits, Flowers, and Foliage

Monica Moran Brandies

B. B. Mackey Books
Wayne, Pennsylvania

Citrus: How to Grow and Use Citrus Fruits, Flowers, and Foliage

ISBN 978-1-893443-18-1 $16.95 suggested price
B. B. Mackey Books, Publisher
P. O. Box 475
Wayne, PA 19087 USA
www.mackeybooks.com

Visit the publisher's website for more information about our books, disks, and lectures and events from our authors.

Garden books from B. B. Mackey Books include:
Herbs and Spices for Florida Gardens; Questions and Answers for Deep South Gardeners; Florida Gardening: The Newcomer's Survival Manual; A Cutting Garden for Florida; Creating and Planting Garden Troughs; Who Does Your Garden Grow; Best of Green Space: 30 Years of Composted Columns; Bless You for the Gifts; Garden Notes This Year, and more, as listed on the website, www.mackeybooks.com

Library of Congress Cataloging-in-Publication Data

Brandies, Monica Moran, 1938-
Citrus : how to grow and use citrus fruits, flowers, and foliage
Monica Moran Brandies. -- 1st ed.
p. cm.
Includes index.
ISBN 978-1-893443-18-1
1. Citrus. 2. Citrus fruits. I. Title.
SB369.B725 2010
634'.304--dc22
2010042885

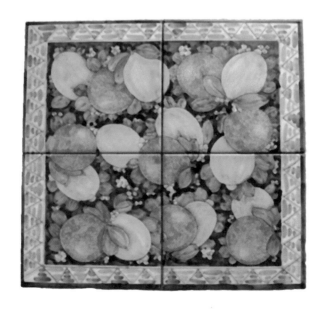

*To David,
my best friend*

Starting with Citrus

Whether you grow citrus trees in containers that spend the winter indoors or live where you can grow oranges and lemons in the ground, you are growing one of the world's most useful, beautiful, bountiful, and longest lasting herbal plants. If you don't grow your own, you will find citrus a good value at your local grocery and at produce stands.

This book will help you understand and appreciate your citrus as never before and use all the parts of the fruits and trees to more advantage, even peels or wood or blossoms. There is a whole world of uses and many are quick and easy.

Yes, any citrus qualifies as a herb. A herb (pronounce *herb* or *erb*) is any plant that has uses additional to being ornamental and producing food. Citrus rates very high in doing both of these things. But the flowers, fruit, skins, and foliage of citrus trees have long been prized for their medicinal properties, flavor in cooking, edible flowers, and pleasing aromas. Aromas from citrus are useful in aromatherapy, perfume, cosmetics, household products, insect repellents, and bee and butterfly attractants.

Ponkan orange sections almost fall out of the skin.

How my interest in this herbal tree grew. I admired citrus fruit when I lived in Iowa. I had seen orange groves on Florida vacations and was amazed at the beauty of the trees, even though I had not yet breathed in the fragrance of the flowers. Though I had only sprouted seeds from fruit with my children, my weekly garden column in Iowa took me to a home where there was a grapefruit tree in the dining room that was as tall as the ceiling. The young sons had started it from seeds and now stood beneath its generous canopy.

We moved to Florida over 23 years ago and now I have 15 different kinds of citrus in my yard. I've long been a member of the Rare Fruit Council International (RFCI) where I've met people who are generous with their large fund of information and inspiration. Until I joined that group I had never heard of a pummelo, but now that tree is the most treasured in my garden with its huge and unique fruit. It is the largest citrus, the grandfather of the grapefruit but sweeter and less acidic.

I had never seen or heard of, let alone eaten, Ponkan or Page oranges, but now I grow them. This is a gardener's dream come true. I am not a citrus expert, simply a home grower who enjoys growing, eating, and drinking the golden apples and their many cousins. I have written two books on herbs, and I am learning to use citrus trees, fruit, and leaves in many herbal ways which will be described in these chapters.

5

History

Long before I could grow oranges, I was fascinated by their part in history. Oranges were considered the fruit of the gods and then the fruit of kings. They were noted in Indochina 5,000 years ago. Their golden color, the beauty of the trees, and the fragrance of the flowers made them greatly coveted. In time caravans carried seeds from the Orient to the Near East and the Persian Empire. They were as high in cost as they were in esteem, rare and sacred. They were used through the ages in fertility rites.

When the Moors brought them to Spain, they were grown in walled gardens and any Christian who touched them risked death. The Moors were driven out 500 years later and they could not take their orange groves with them. Along with sugar, oranges became the most valuable trade goods in Europe.

Perhaps no other plant ever made such a difference in history, because its availability coincided with the time of Columbus and the great voyages of discovery. The fact that citrus can be kept a long time and prevents scurvy and other diseases from malnutrition made possible the age of exploration. And the ships' captains saw to the planting of citrus seeds in every port where the climate was suitable.

When Christopher Columbus returned from his first voyage with little to show for his venture, he was glad to tell Isabella and Ferdinand that he had found rich lands and a gentle climate for sugar and orange plantations. On his second crossing, he brought seeds and plants that would be needed for a colony including oranges and sugar cane. Planted first on the island of Hispaniola, now Haiti and the Dominican Republic, they grew very well.

Pummelos followed a similar route of migration and were found in Spain and Israel by the late twelfth century. Grapefruit, probably a mutation of pummelo, was noted in Barbados by the eighteenth century.

While new varieties of oranges, grapefruits, tangerines, and such have been developed, sour oranges are still grown commercially for marmalade, flavoring, candies, and fragrant oil for perfume and drinks. In France the most delicate and fragrant perfumes come from the flowers of which a single bitter orange tree averages sixty-six pounds.

Worldwide, there is more citrus grown than all the apples, peaches, pears, plums, and other deciduous fruits put together. And because of the commercial aspect that has shaped the history of the orange bowl states, plant breeders continue to develop new and superior varieties for flavor, disease resistance, profusion of fruit, cold hardiness, and a wide range of ripening times.

Citrus groves have had to face and overcome new diseases and problems that seem to have accelerated in the present day. Paul Harris, whose Harris Citrus Nursery in Lithia, Florida, grows nearly 100 different kinds of citrus, is convinced that nothing will destroy either the citrus industry or the homeowners satisfaction in this most amazing herbal tree.

Buying and Storing Citrus Fruits

If you cannot or do not grow citrus, you can buy many varieties in the grocery and at fruit and vegetable stands. Choose fruits that seem heavy for their size and have good, bright colored skins. There are some varieties that are ripe and delicious even when still green. Valencias sometimes go back to green in warm weather but are ripe and good. Avoid fruit with bruised or wrinkled skin.

Unfortunately you can not taste an orange before you buy it as you can a grape from the clump, but when you find a variety you have not tried before, buy a small amount and see how you like it. The citrus selection chapter starting on page 53 will help.

Oranges vary in size and shape and some that look strange, like the Ponkans, are the most delicious. So look around and taste so that you don't miss that treasure. Do not be concerned with russetting, a mottling of brown or tan on the skins. This often indicates thin skin and superior quality. Oranges will keep well for a week at room temperature (best for juice) or at least a month, possibly as long as six to eight weeks in the refrigerator or in a cool but not freezing place. This applies to most citrus.

Lemons should be smooth with small points on each end.

Limes can vary in color from bright green to pale yellow. Key limes will be smaller and rounder. Limes will keep in the refrigerator for two weeks and at room temperature for one week.

Grapefruits should have a firm, smooth skin, the color of which will vary some depending on the color inside. The sweetest ones I've ever tasted had skin almost red. These will keep for a month in the refrigerator.

If you find a pummelo, buy and try it. It is delicious. You can eat it right away or keep it on a shelf for two weeks or more and it just gets sweeter. These come in different sizes and shapes, mostly large, and some are bell shaped.

Tangerines come in many sizes and shapes and usually are a bit smaller than oranges and with naturally looser skin. They will keep in the refrigerator for several weeks.

If you live in a citrus growing climate and someone offers you fruit, take at least a few and try them. There are many delicious kinds that do not store or ship well and are never found otherwise.

Easy Trees to Grow

If you live where citrus trees grow outdoors, you are fortunate. Consider them first for your landscaping scheme. Many are ideal small dooryard trees, lovely in all seasons. Some of the grapefruits will grow tall enough to frame a home. On all, the leaves are evergreen and glossy. The flowers bloom for almost a month with a heavenly fragrance that spreads through the neighborhood. The fruits set on in the spring and stay green until the fall and winter. A few, like the grapefruit, kumquats, and pummelos, hang fresh and prime on the tree for many months so you don't have to process or store them. Just pick and eat as needed.

Grafted trees. You may, in time, get some good citrus from seeds and that worked well in places where time and space were of no consideration. But only the pummelo and the key lime will come true from seeds and they can take 15 years or more to produce fruit. With the others you wait all those years and then may well not like the taste or size. So buying grafted plants of citrus is the only sensible solution for the homeowner who has limited space and an eagerness for delicious fruit.

You may be tempted by what are sometimes called "fruit cocktail" trees, grafted with several different kinds of citrus. The larger fruits tend to take over such a tree eventually. The experts in the Rare Fruit Council recommend planting up to three different trees in the same hole if space is limited. That way, each kind has its own trunk and root system and the smaller fruits have a better chance for equal abundance.

Fruit season. Oranges come in three different groups depending on when they ripen: early winter, mid to late winter, and the Valencias that ripen from March until June in Florida, March to October in parts of California, and hang among the blossoms. In ideal circumstances, a single orange tree can produce 1400 oranges. Okay, mine don't, but they keep us in juice and fresh fruit all winter and for at least seven months of the year.

Sun and shade. Citrus does best in full sun. I planted mine in full sun. Then the oak trees overgrew and now overshadow them, but we still get an amazing amount of fruit. Citrus is one of the fruit trees most tolerant of some shade and when we have a cold spell, the shade is worth a few degrees of warmth that may well save the fruit or even the tree.

Hardiness. The fruit is hardy down to at least 28 degrees F. We had some nights down to 26, but our fruit survived. In the freeze of Christmas,

8

1989, my trees were young and not yet bearing, but the temperature went down to 18 degrees F. One of my grapefruit trees came back from the rootstock as a sour orange. During cold spells, the most important part to cover is from a foot above the graft point to the ground. This can usually be done with mulch, though groves have Styrofoam "bandages" to cover that area of young trees. The older the tree, the more cold hardy it becomes.

Michael Kesinger, Bureau Chief of the Florida Bureau of Citrus Budwood Registration for the Plant Industry, says that in 1980 it was not unusual to find a citrus tree 100 years old and still bearing, but since then diseases have increased and few trees last that long.

Still, citrus trees are easy for the homeowner to grow, much easier than the peaches, apples,

This kumquat tree grows in a conservatory

and cherries I grew in the north. The biggest need here in central Florida's sandy soil is for soil amendment at planting time and thereafter. I was told not to mulch citrus and it took me a long time to learn that is because trees are susceptible to root rot from excess dampness which comes with our rainy summers. Since I have long been convinced that mulch is the best thing I can do for any of my plants, I do mulch my citrus the rest of the year, being careful to keep the mulch away from the trunk and to rake it back before the summer rains. I figure the mulch does more good than the risk involved.

It is important to water any newly set trees deeply until they are settled. Citrus likes to dry out between waterings. Once settled I water mine only during very dry times (April and May) and then deeply every other week.

Feeding Citrus Trees

During the first year, starting about four to six weeks after planting, apply half a pound of 6-6-6 with added minor elements or citrus fertilizer every six weeks from March through September. Sprinkle this in a wide circle starting about six inches from the trunk and extending out to slightly beyond the drip line, the edge of the leaf spread.

During the next two years, use a full pound for every year the tree has been planted and apply on the same schedule. For the first three years, do not use anything stronger than 8-8-8.

Nocatee tangelos

After three years, feed three times a year in mid February, June and early October, with citrus fertilizer or you can use a balanced formula up to 10-10-10. Measure around the circumference of the trunk six inches above the ground and use half a pound for each inch of circumference to a maximum of 20 pounds per feeding. Since the rains usually start in mid June in Florida and can leach away and contaminate the ground water, you may want to make two smaller applications.

Organic fertilizer is preferable but expensive if you have many trees, and it can be hard to find. If you have only one or two trees, it would be worthwhile. Owners of organic groves use natural limestone and gypsum, a rock phosphate mixture that includes many of the necessary trace elements, and often plant cover crops in the grove and chop them throughout the year for green manure. Home growers find a foliar feeding with fish emulsion to be helpful and can also use aged animal manures, but will still need something to give the trees enough phosphorus and potassium.

I am careful to not to use chemical pesticides, but I use chemical fertilizers and still have a great population of earthworms from all the mulch and compost I have added. I consider this an indication that the fertilizer is not doing harm to them.

Plant Purchases and Pruning

You don't have to buy special dwarf trees. Most types of the citrus stay low and can easily be topped or sheared to keep them in bounds. Their size depends largely on which rootstock they are on, the ones on 'Flying Dragon' being the smallest. Besides the taste and variety, consider rootstocks if there is a large citrus grower selling trees in your area. These determine the size of the tree, the disease resistance, hardiness and adaptation to soil type such as acid or alkaline. If you buy from retail growers, you won't have much choice of rootstock and must depend on their selection. But I can go to Harris Nursery in Lithia, Florida, and tell them what I want in size and hardiness, and they help me choose from a much larger base.

I have my trees topped whenever the tree trimmers come (every three to five years) mostly because it is difficult to reach above a certain height for picking. Other than that, I only prune out dead wood or any that is crossing the path.

You do need to watch for shoots coming up from below the graft point and keep these pruned off or they will take over the tree with an inferior variety. Only one of my trees is determined to do this and I have to prune those shoots constantly. The other trees rarely send up rootstock shoots.

Most homeowners don't spray at all (I haven't sprayed yet in my 23 years of growing), though commercial growers are fighting more and more diseases. They are also coming up with more resistant varieties and rootstocks, so if we do lose a tree, we can confidently replant another. I am still in awe of how fast citrus, indeed all trees, grow in our semi-tropical climate.

If you buy the smallest grafted trees, it may take two or three years to get fruit. If you buy a tree in a three gallon pot, sometimes with fruit already on it, you will have fruit from the first season and more with each season that comes. But don't let a young tree produce too much fruit or it will not make good vegetative growth.

Finding and Growing Good Citrus Trees

Citrus fruits vary in taste, aroma, color, texture, and shape mostly because of the variety you plant. But there are also differences that arise from your location and the season. The same varieties may vary in growth, time of ripening, and appearance if they are grown in Florida rather than California, and there are variations even between coastal and inland California. In his fascinating book, *Oranges*, John McPhee explains this: "The annual difference in rainfall between the Florida and California orange growing areas is one million one hundred and forty thousand gallons per acre." And irrigation can only do so much.

On the same tree the fruit growing on the outside is sweeter than that growing on the inside, and higher growing fruit is sweeter than lower, because of the amount of sun. Oranges growing on the south side of the tree are the sweetest, then those on the east and west, and least sweet are those on the north side. The amount of juice and of Vitamin C varies accordingly.

Even in the same individual fruit the blossom end half is sweeter than the stem end. But all of it is so good!

Choose varieties that thrive in your area. Wherever you live and can grow citrus outdoors, I'd suggest you at once plant at least one larger tree (such as one in a three gallon container with some fruit already on it), to get some fruit quickly. The higher cost of

These are willowleaf mandarin oranges. The blossom end is always at the bottom.

11

the tree will be offset by the almost immediate harvest. Select a variety that you have tasted.

The best place to get these trees is from a citrus grower if there is one in your area. Some wholesalers will sell only in large lots, but when I asked Paul Harris how many trees one needed to buy to come directly to their nursery for them, he answered, "At least one." If your nearest wholesaler does not handle retail sales, he may give you a list of nurseries that carry his trees.

Members of RFCI cut up fruit in preparation for the tasting.

RFCI. You can find good quality, selection, and information at any sale involving the Rare Fruit Council International (RFCI). That is where I got most of my trees. There was a time when I would have said to avoid the big franchise outlets, but now I know some great local growers who grow especially for them. I'd still ask the stores where they get their trees. Some sell plants that are not appropriate to our climate.

Once you get that first tree growing, do some homework. There are chapters of RFCI all over the world and visitors are welcome at meetings. The members include beginners and experts and they are some of the nicest people you will ever meet. Go to meetings. Join. Read and save the newsletters. Ask questions. Our group (Tampa Bay), as one member says, "has more fun that God ought to allow," and has a tasting table at every meeting that is worth double the dues. If you can't get to meetings, you can still learn a great deal just from the newsletters.

Florida Citrus Arboretum. With great delight, my husband, who is my best encourager, and I visited the Florida Citrus Arboretum where they have over 250 varieties on six and a half acres. It is located at 3027 Lake Alfred Road, which is US 17, in Winter Haven and is open to the public Monday through Friday from 9 am to 4 pm from October 1 until March 1. For a very reasonable payment ($5 in 2010) they will give you a half a bushel bag that you can fill with the varieties that tempt you most. You might want to separate them in smaller plastic bags within the half bushel bag and mark the bags or write on the rind the names of the varieties. The smaller bags also allow for easier carrying. Most of the fruit will ripen from November until March, so for best picking and observing, go early in winter. This facility is part of the state's Bureau of Citrus Budwood Registration. For information, call 863-298-7712.

I went back again with my young friend, Eric Young, for whom it was part of his home schooling, and we had another wonderful day. This kind of homework is most enjoyable.

In California. If you are in southern California, you'll want to see the California Citrus State Historic Park, a newer and larger facility that shows an old-time citrus producing community and has a large collections of citrus varieties and a view of citrus groves. It is located on Van Buren Boulevard at Dufferin Ave., in Riverside (92504). It's roughly half way between Los Angeles and Palm Springs. Call 951-780-6222.

In Florida. Our RFCI group has an annual Citrus Tasting on the first or second Sunday in February at the Florida State Fair in Tampa where people can taste a wide range of various citrus varieties, all cut up into bite size pieces. At the last one when we were worried about finding enough citrus, there were 72 different varieties plus eight other fruits to taste for a dollar a plate. At this event, at meetings, and at RFCI sales, you will find members willing and eager to answer your questions about their favorite varieties and how to grow and use them.

Friends in Fort Myers look forward to the day after Thanksgiving when their paper comes in a special bag from Sun Harvest Citrus offering all the citrus they can put in that bag for free to anyone who makes a purchase. When packing such a bag, mix large fruits like grapefruit with small ones like tangerines to fill every space. "When we check out, they can't believe we could get so much in that bag," Perry Penniston says.

Your County Extension Service will have free information on the varieties recommended for your area. This service is one of the best uses of our tax money and the more I learn, the more I call on them with questions. I could not do without them.

Grocery stores are starting to carry more variety, but produce stands are the best bet for tasting and buying the less common kinds of citrus. The more tasting you do, the better you can select the varieties you will enjoy.

Hardiness

Citrus fruits range in cold hardiness for the fruit from Key lime as the most likely to be damaged up through lemon, grapefruit, orange, mandarin to kumquat as the hardiest.

But the trees themselves do not follow the same order. Most kumquat trees will survive down to 20 F; then sour orange, Meyer lemon (24 to 25 F); most mandarins, sweet oranges, the majority of which are hardy to 26 or 27 F; then tangelo, pummelos and grapefruit are the least hardy. Damage also depends on how quickly the cold comes down, how long it lasts, and the maturity of the tree and the fruit. Young trees are much more sensitive to cold than older ones.

There are also microclimates in your yard that will protect them better than others. Trees under some shade will produce less in a single year but may live longer to produce much more over all because the shade gives two to three degrees more protection from freezing.

A nearby body of water is a great help. The larger the better, but even our above-ground pool made the area a little warmer, and that led me to surround it with marginally hardy plants. By the time we removed the pool, many were mature enough to keep on growing and producing.

The Sex Life of Citrus

Most citrus trees, with the exception of a few of the mandarins, do not need two trees for pollination. In fact, some satsumas and navels do not always need pollination but will set fruit from flowers that aren't fertilized,

grapefruit blossom

and the fruit is therefore seedless. Most citrus trees will still set fruit, but definitely will set more fruit, up to four times more, when bees are there to help with pollination. Commercial growers often have bee hives shipped in for bloom time. Homeowners learn to "Plant it and they will come," but beekeepers have had terrible setbacks from Colony Collapse Disorder and there are fewer bees out there. So it is more important than ever to use as few poisonous chemicals as possible and to plant other bee attracting plants such as cosmos, marigolds, zinnias, geraniums, heirloom roses, squash, pumpkins, gourds, lavender, bee balm, sage, mints, thyme, and fennel and flowering trees and shrubs to feed the bees for the rest of the year.

Growing Citrus in Colder Climates

If you live where you cannot grow citrus outdoors, there are certain kinds that will do well in containers, especially if you have bright light indoors for winter and you can move them outdoors to full sun for the summer. You may not get much fruit, but you will have a lovely plant, fragrant flowers, an unusual conversation piece, and some fruit to enjoy.

Select the hardiest kinds: lemons, limes, kumquats (Meiwa is sweet and delicious), and calamondin (sour but good for jam) and 'Owari' Satsuma mandarins. Almost any type grown on Flying Dragon rootstocks will do well in large containers such as half whisky barrels. The search for more cold-hardy varieties is rapidly progressing. Citrus 'Yuza' is a shrubby natural mandarin hybrid with mildly sweet, lemony flavored fruit that is hardy as low as 10 F (-12 C) or lower. The 'Thomasville' orangequat

14

is a small tree with lime like fruit that is hardy to about 0 F (-18 C). Citrus 'Morton' and 'US-119' taste much like a tart orange and are supposedly hardy to 5 F (-15 C) or below.

Depending on where you live, you may have to get your trees from a catalog. Another option is to get your friends in orange country to start a few cuttings for you before you visit. Citrus cuttings are not easy to root, but there is about a 50 percent chance of success if placed under a plastic bag and a better chance with a misting system. Dennis Gretton tells me that these cuttings will make a nice shrub but never a tree because they do not have a rootstock. But for a container and as a mostly ornamental plant that would not matter. And the lack of cost would make the effort worthwhile. I wouldn't try seedlings because they will take so long to bloom and bear, but cuttings would not.

Sour oranges are said to be excellent for containers and I know they are gung ho to grow wherever they can. They are also very decorative. On our last trip to the Arboretum we decided that the variegated sour orange 'Panache' and the 'Bouquet de Fleurs' were the loveliest trees there, loaded with blossoms and fruit at the same time.

Sour orange
'Bouquet de Fleurs'

When moving container citrus plants indoors and out, make slow transitions over at least three or four weeks. When moving plants outdoors, keep them covered for a decreasing part of the day until they adjust to both the light and the temperature change. Before bringing them indoors, start reducing the light gradually a month before the first expected frost. If you do not do this, the leaves will fall like rain when they come indoors. Do not water before moving them for it will greatly increase the weight of the plants. And wait for help rather than risk muscle strain.

Most plants prefer cooler temperatures and higher humidity that most homes offer. A greenhouse is best if kept above freezing. A cool sunroom is next best. A humidifier will help, but even with that you should mist the leaves often and surround the plant with pebble-filled trays of water that will increase the humidity around the leaves as the water evaporates.

Water less in winter and allow soil to dry out between waterings. Fertilize **very** lightly indoors until four weeks before the spring move. Provide plenty of light by growing them within six feet of a sunny window or with artificial light during the daytime only. Provide up to 50 percent extra humidity with trays of pebbles and frequent misting of foliage. Keep plants away from drafts and heat sources. If plants bloom inside with no

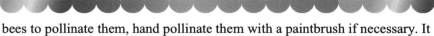

bees to pollinate them, hand pollinate them with a paintbrush if necessary. It depends on the variety.

Citrus in the Kitchen

Citrus flowers are all edible. Just pull them off the tree, wash them gently, let them dry a few minutes on a clean paper or cloth towel, and then add them to salads, teas, or soups. Or let them dry to keep for future use.

Of course, you don't want to strip the tree of all the flowers that might turn into fruit, but nature provides many extras. Take a few from several bunches rather than a whole bunch from one place.

Citrus fruit eaten whole and fresh is low calorie, fat free, cholesterol free, refined sugar free, fiber rich, and loaded with important vitamins and minerals as well as being delicious.

Citrus and related fruits will not ripen after being picked, but they will stay in prime condition on the tree for many weeks or months, depending on the variety and barring a freeze that goes below 28 degrees F. If cold weather forces you to pick more than you can use, fruit will keep for several weeks in a cool place. Otherwise, leave fruits on the tree until needed or as long as they are in prime condition.

This requires knowing what variety you have and the months its season for picking covers. Do not depend on the color. Some kinds like the Ponkan, Oroblanco, and Satsuma can be ready when they are still mostly green. Valencias are orange months before they are sweet and sometimes get lighter or even turn back to lime green when fully ripe. Taste is the test.

If you lost the tag or never knew the variety name, or if you got the fruiting trees with the property and don't know the kinds, you will have to taste and learn by experience.

If you notice that wildlife is eating your fruit, you can be sure it is ready. Animals know to the day. The trick is to get there a day ahead. We have an outdoor cat that keeps wildlife from becoming much of a problem. We hardly ever see varmints among our fruit, though sometimes we can tell they were there in the night from the partially eaten fruit on the ground. Sometimes the birds eat holes in the fruit while it still hangs on the trees, but not much is damaged for us.

How to Harvest Citrus

When you pick citrus, take hold of the fruit and give it a quick twist. Some types, especially tangerines, are best cut off. If picking opens up a hole at the stem end, use that fruit quickly or it will rot.

Pick the larger fruits first because they tend to dry out toward the end of their season, especially the navel oranges. They are still good, but not nearly as juicy. I pick the tangerines on the side away from the window first because I so enjoy looking out and seeing those loaded limbs.

My husband fixed a claw type cultivator onto a longer pole with masking tape so we can reach the tops of the trees to rake off the high fruits. You can also buy harvesting poles that include a basket lined with a sponge for catching the fruit. Only the pummelos seem to split from a high fall, and they won't fit into those catchers. Use a ladder for them if necessary. They are well worth the trouble.

Our little grandsons like to help us pick, and since they are closer to the ground, they save us much stooping. They devised their own way to eat the

thin skinned tangerines. They bite or poke a hole and squeeze the juice right into their mouths.

Pummelos and Grapefruit All Winter

Our two grapefruit trees, one pink and one white, kept my father supplied for his morning breakfast until he died at age 101.

The pummelo, also spelled pommelo or pomelo, is the largest citrus. Some fruits get as large as ten inches in diameter and weigh several pounds. The pummelo tree is the ancestor of the grapefruit. My tree is probably a Hirado Butan with pink flesh that tastes somewhat like grapefruit but sweeter, drier, and less acid. There are at least 20 varieties of pummelo, several with a pear shape including Siamese Pink, Sha Tian You, and Sun Hing. Some have pink flesh, some white. Red Shaddock, named after the East Indian ship captain believed to have brought the seeds to Barbados in about 1700, has dark red flesh and is an excellent juicy fruit. Tahitian has greenish white flesh with a tart, lime like flavor.

We pick from our tree from November to May and the fruits can sit on a shelf for a few weeks and will get sweeter. I had one that sat for two months. The skin turned soft and bumpy, then hard as a shell, but it was the sweetest one we'd ever eaten. I have also had them go soft after a few weeks. If you notice this happening, cut out the bad part out at once and eat the rest. It will still be good.

I find the taste of pummelo superior to grapefruit, but my father disagreed. It is harder to prepare since the membranes are tougher. Even from the same tree, some have a thick rind and pith and some do not.

For best eating plain or in salads, cut off a slice at both ends, then remove the rest of the peel and pith, separate the segments, and remove the pulp from the casings. Discard the seeds. Pummelos, like most citrus fruits, tend to be seedier if grown near other citrus, less so if grown in isolation. Mine are not overly seedy.

If pummelo fruit sits around too long after you have prepared it for eating it gets bitter, possibly because the metal of the knife reacts with the fruit. If you cut the outer skin with the metal knife but dissect the sections with a plastic picnic knife, the flavor stays sweet. If you cut one in half or quarter and take out all the fruit not surrounded by membrane, you can put the rest in the refrigerator to keep for a few more days.

You can also freeze segments of any citrus fruit in its own juice in plastic or glass containers and it tastes as sweet and delicious as fresh when thawed. You can even freeze whole grapefruits. When they thaw, the skin is soft and the flavor a bit more tart than fresh and the fruit extra juicy, but it still tastes good. You can sweeten it with a teaspoon or less of white or brown sugar, honey, or pancake syrup.

If you have fruit that you won't be using, bag it up and take it to church or to work and set it out with a "Help Yourself" sign and it will all find a good home. Or give it to a food pantry for the needy. Citrus, especially homegrown, is too good to let go to waste.

Making Juice

When we moved to Florida we soon found that we could buy freshly squeezed juice from local groves and their outlets. The taste is great but juice tastes even better when it comes from your own trees.

If you live where you can grow citrus, you will find that some oranges are too good for juice, and eating the whole orange gives you fiber and other good things that you'd miss if you only drink your oranges. We eat most of the Ponkans out of hand or give them to the many people who hesitated to taste them when they were first ripe but still green, but found out how good they are. They are so good one can eat several at a sitting, or standing over the sink. One man said the Ponkan was the only citrus he could peel and

eat while driving, but even with Ponkan I don't recommend that.

We also eat most of the navels whole. If sliced in half from top to bottom and then cut into sections, they can make a snack. Navel juice and blood orange juice are said to have a much shorter shelf life than most but we use both when we are squeezing for drinking fresh.

For the best taste and nutrition, squeeze only what you will use at once or within 24 to 48 hours. Or you can make larger batches less often and put what you will drink in one to three days into the refrigerator. Fill the other plastic or glass containers with a little room for expansion at the top, perhaps 1 ½ inches per half gallon, and keep them in the freezer until needed. Since there are no preservatives, not even the natural ones in the whole fruit, pure juice has a short shelf life.

If you find your juice going bitter sooner, be careful not to press too hard when juicing. Remember that the white pith has a bitter flavor.

Now we have oranges and grapefruits ripening from November until we use the last of the Valencias sometimes as late as June. When we first began to harvest, there was a county cannery that had a juicing machine. We'd save containers over the summer, clear off a shelf in the freezer, pick a bushel or more of oranges, and head for the cannery where a charming lady helped us through the process: washing the fruit and the containers, watching the machine squeeze the juice, and bottling it from a faucet-like spigot. It cost very little and saved much time. Unfortunately, the cannery closed due to lack of use. So we have become good at squeezing at home.

Fruit at room temperature will yield a bit more juice than cold fruit. I used to wash each fruit in a sink of water with just a tad of dish soap. Now I spread the fruit on the shelves of my dishwasher and put it through the "rinse only" nine-minute cycle. Then I dry it on the counter covered with a clean towel. Some people don't wash the fruit if it seems clean right off the tree.

Roll the fruit on a hard surface to soften it and make the juice easier to extract. We get more juice when picking just after a good rain and sweeter juice after the first cold spell.

Our citrus trees are in some shade and therefore produce less than that possible 400 pounds each. But we drink about a gallon of orange juice a week, and in a good year have fresh squeezed juice from November until July from the six to eight juice trees in full production.

While orange juice from the store must come from oranges only unless labeled otherwise, at home we mix oranges and tangerines, or oranges and grapefruit, or whatever combinations we like. We have one blood orange tree whose fruits we mix with the Valencia for a juice that is dark red and delicious. Sometimes we buy a bag labeled "juice oranges" for a new mix.

Grapefruit juice versus fruit. There are warnings about combining grapefruit and certain medications. One doctor told his patients that half a grapefruit won't hurt as long as you separate the eating from the pill by several hours, e.g. grapefruit for breakfast, medication at bedtime. But this does not, he said, apply to grapefruit juice because a single glass may contain the juice from one or even two grapefruits. My husband checked with his doctor and his said a half a fresh grapefruit was fine even at the same time as the pills. Check with you own doctor on this.

One grower in Lakeland reported people coming to get his navel grapefruit because it is lower in acid and less likely to give trouble with medicines. I don't take those medicines, so I squeeze a few grapefruits at the end of each orange squeezing. This juice helps me control my appetite.

Use all the juice. You can use citrus juice to season chicken, steak, pork chops or fish or to fire up a stir fry. It adds flavor and nutrition to muffins, cakes, and breads and even pies. Any extras will make a good orange wine.

Dried Oranges

When I juice Satsuma mandarin oranges, the sections quickly fall right out of the skins and stick to the bulb of the juicer. They are much too good to throw away, so some of them I eat as I work and they are delicious. I put the rest in a jar. When the jar is filled, I pour a bit of the juice back over them and eat them the next day or so or put them in the freezer if there is more than one jar.

Then I thought of drying them. People dry tomatoes, so why not oranges? Sometimes I spread the Satsuma sections, already minus most of the seeds and juice, onto a cookie sheet covered with waxed paper. I give them about one hour in the evening at the lowest setting the oven will provide and another hour the next morning, and then they are ready to fill the dried orange jar.

dried Satsumas

Leave the oven door open about three inches while drying anything so the moisture can escape.

After soaking the dried oranges for a few hours in water or orange juice, they are good in cookies or cakes. My sister Anne has a recipe for Craisin Oatmeal Cookies that calls for the dried cranberries to soak in orange juice, so she added some of the dried oranges and the cookies were even more delicious and nutritious.

The dried Satsumas are not bad as snacks, not quite delicious, but if we are ever hungry or caught without power after a hurricane, or maybe just in the summer when citrus is scarce, they will suddenly seem more tasty. I have not yet tried drying other varieties.

If the cook is happy and healthy, so is the family.

Navel oranges are notorious for drying on the trees and even when they are juicy, much pulp is left in the skin after juicing. So I juice some with the rest of my mix even when there is very little juice. Then I cut the halves in half, turn the pieces inside out and scrape the pulp into a glass or plastic container (used yogurt cups are great) and cover the pulp with the mixed juice. This I let set for a few hours or overnight in the refrigerator and eat with a spoon. You could also mix in sliced bananas, strawberries, or many other fruits as desired. Canned fruit cocktail can't hold a candle to this. Or add it to fruit salads. Delicious! I call it Ambrosia. My husband says, "What are you eating for breakfast? Sludge again?" Don't worry if all of your family doesn't appreciate all my ideas. Just use the ones that appeal to them or to you. If the cook is happy and healthy, so is the family.

Lemon Juice

Lemon juice will keep foods such as apples, pears, and avocados, even in guacamole, from losing their color between slicing and serving. This may not be necessary if you are adding salad dressing at once. We used to use lemon juice when we were freezing peaches so they wouldn't turn dark.

Keep Lemon Juice on Hand. Freeze lemon juice in ice trays and store the cubes in freezer bags , frozen for individual portions. Each cube equals about two tablespoons of lemon juice.

Lemon or lime sections are often added to plates of fish because lemon juice enhances the flavor of fish and other foods too. Citrus makes food more appetizing in low-sodium diets. Use it on melons to bring out flavor.

Squeeze lemon juice over cooked vegetables and raw fruit to preserve their appealing color.

Citrus Zest

Citrus peels are famous for flavoring. Ann Uual tells of a friend who always asked if she wanted to have lemon sponge cake or orange sponge cake. When she decided, the hostess grated the requested rind into the batter.

Evelyn Hamilton remembers that her mother always peeled an orange round and round in one piece and kept the curly strip on a hook in the kitchen where it dried. "She did not have a grater but she'd cut that peel with a kitchen shears into tiny pieces and used it, especially on sweet potato souffle and other sweet potato dishes. We grew our own sweet potatoes, so she used it often," she says.

Grated citrus rind is aptly called *zest* for it can be used to add flavor and zest to many recipes from meat to muffins, curries to cakes. The colored part of the rind, called the *flavedo*, is very rich in aromatic oils and is used to add unique flavors to recipes. Try to avoid getting any of the white inner rind, the *albedo*, in with the zest because it tends to have a bitter taste, though is otherwise harmless and indeed rich in vitamin C.

Choose fruit that is free of pesticides, wax, dyes and blemishes. Wash and dry it well. Grate or peel for zest before juicing or eating the fruit. One average orange will yield about 1 tablespoon of zest, one large orange 2 tablespoons. Limes vary according to the thickness of their flavedo, but Key limes are too thin-skinned for zest. I was surprised to learn that fruit with pebbly skin rather than smooth gives the best zest.

Kieffer or Kaffir Limes

The Kieffir or Kaffir lime, *Citrus hystrix*, the leaves of which are used in Thai cooking, is excellent for zest though the fruit itself is too sour to be edible. The leaves have a winged petiole or stem that looks like a leaf with

two elongated sections. They have a very pungent taste that can be overwhelming, so use this, as you would any herb, in small amounts until you know how and how much you and your family will like it. The Thais remove the midrib of the leaf and cut the remaining parts into very thin slices or

shred them to use as a garnish on salads or mixed into curries. Having a fresh leaf is ideal, but they can also be frozen for up to a year.

Zesting tools and methods. There are specialized tools for zesting. One is called a citrus zester or canelle or channel knife and it has tiny holes that cut shallow ribbons from the skin. It is also has a canelle blade built into the side of the head for decorating fruit and vegetables by cutting away a thin strip of the skin to leave an interesting shape or pattern. Besides citrus, it can also be used on carrots, cucumbers, radishes, apples, pears, lemons, firm bananas, etc. The strips removed can be curled and added to drinks or cocktails or for food decoration.

For even finer shreds, there is the **microplane grater.** This long, thin grater with a handle can also be used for grating chocolate, hard cheese,  coconut, ginger and garlic, so you may have one already or be glad to get one if you are a gourmet cook.

I am a very plain cook after years of cooking for a family of ten (our last child was not born until after the older ones had left home) who cared more for quantity and taste than fine details. So I am glad to tell you that you can just use a paring knife or potato peeler, being careful not to go into the albedo. With the grater, use the side with smallest holes. To clean the grater afterward, a dry pastry brush will help.

It is best to use the zest fresh, but any extra can be dried and even put into a salt shaker to use as a condiment. Dried zest can also be used in beauty and household products. To dry zest, spread it on a clean screen or paper towel and air dry it near a sunny window. Indoors will take three to five days. You can also use a food dryer.

After is it dry, it should be ground to the consistency of ground coffee and this can be done in a coffee grinder, in a food processor, or with a mortar and pestle. Store the dry ground zest in an airtight container and label it. Use within one to three months. Like any herb, dried is more potent than fresh, so use half as much and check for taste.

Use finely ground zest with tea blends (it is already in Earl Grey teas), in place of an extract in baking, or to flavor sugar, honey, or barbecue sauce.

Remove the zest before you juice or eat the fruit. Chop it and freeze it right away. It is not necessary to thaw it before using, but because you may get some ice crystals, it is best to add a little more than you would of fresh zest. It will keep well in the freezer for six months, which will carry you to the next citrus season.

Citrus as Garnish

A slice of lemon in a glass of water not only adds flavor, but eye appeal. Perhaps this is meant to purify and improve the flavor of the water served. Whole orange slices used as garnish on plates add an air of abundance and color. Slices for garnish should be 1/8 to 1/4 inch thick for lemons or limes, 1/4 of an inch for oranges. To make a more decorative garnish, take the citrus slice and cut the circle from rind to center, pull the edges apart, and twist the ends in opposite directions.

I have a Meiwa kumquat, the sweet one, planted between the front door and the mailbox. It is a small and lovely tree and we eat the small fruits skin and all. Kumquats also make delicious jam (p. 27) and are good candied or pickled as a tasty garnish. You can slice them as an edible decoration on salads or deserts, or put two on a toothpick with a lemon round for drinks. Calamondins can be peeled and frozen and used as ice cubes in drinks.

I don't know what the etiquette is for eating garnishes, but I abhor waste and usually eat the orange garnishes before the plates are collected. I don't care for lemons plain, but carry a plastic sandwich bag in my purse to bring them home for one of their many other uses. Citrus, mint, and parsley will clean both the palate and the breath after a meal.

Fruit Pomanders

In Ohio, years ago, we studded oranges with cloves and floated them in punch bowls of hot apple cider. The whole room smelled wonderful. It takes time and many cloves to stud the oranges. The least expensive way is to buy whole cloves in bulk from a natural foods store. The ones with the largest heads and strongest stems will work best. Figure on one ounce per average sized orange and use simple lines and designs rather than a solid covering. Before starting, squeeze the fruit gently to soften the skin. You still may need to use a darning needle to start the holes for the stems. You can also use smaller fruit such as calamondin oranges, lemon or limequats or some of the larger kumquats.

Leave one clove space between each pair to allow for shrinkage as the fruit dries. Also leave a strip around the fruit for a ribbon so the fruit can be hung later. Display the pomanders in a bowl or basket with evergreen foliage as a centerpiece while the fruit dries (it darkens to a brownish color), then hang them in the closet or put them in drawers.

Recipes

Once when we were gleaning for the Society of St. Andrew, we picked citrus from a large grove. We passed the owner's house as we went in, and he had one tree protected by a small plastic greenhouse. I had to know what that tree was, so I knocked on the door and asked him.

"It is my Key lime," he said. "If you stop on your way out I will give you some juice and my recipe for pie." Since he seemed sincerely happy I'd stopped to ask, I stopped again. The juice had been frozen. The recipe is so simple that my sister Anne made the pie in her motel room kitchenette. There may or may not be more delicious recipes, certainly there are more complicated ones, but we found this one quite good, especially in a chocolate crumb crust.

Mr. Bryant's Easy Key Lime Pie
Juice of 8 Key limes or ½ cup juice
1 can Eagle Brand sweetened condensed milk
1 8 oz. tub of Cool Whip
Mix all together. Put in baked or crumb pie shell and chill. Serve with more whipped topping sprinkled with zest.
Key lime pie is Florida's signature dessert. Legend is that the canned milk used in the pie is the reason it was so popular in the Keys, since they had few fresh milk sources in the late 1800's and early 1900's.

Citrus/Arugula Salad
One of my favorite salads contains arugula leaves, orange or pummelo pieces and/or ripe papaya, a few chopped nuts, and a celery seed or poppy seed dressing. You can buy dressing or make your own.

Celery Seed Dressing
Combine the following in your blender or food processor.
2/3 cup sugar
1 teaspoon dry mustard
1 teaspoon salt
1 small onion, grated
½ cup vinegar
Blend, then add 1 cup salad oil. Mix well. Add 1 teaspoon celery seed. Stir before each use. This is also good on any fruit or tossed salad.

Waldorf Salad and Variations
We are very fond of Waldorf salad–apples, carrots, celery, grapes, raisins, and nuts in a dressing of 3 parts mayonnaise, 1 part sugar, and 1 part vinegar. After we visited friends who added strawberries, I began to add them, too. I just cut up the ones I had picked and frozen. (We live very near the Plant City strawberry fields.) I have also since added pummelo pieces and fruit from my jars, either fresh or frozen. And it tastes just as good as the original and gives a nice variation from season to season. It also is easier to make more, since the citrus is already cut up.

Citrus Combos. There are various ways to combine citrus with seafood, chicken, and pasta and vegetables such as green beans, broccoli, carrots, peas, cucumbers, and peppers. As with all herbs, it is best to start with adding a moderate amount to recipes your family already enjoys.

salmon pummelo dinner

Salmon and Pummelo Seafood Supper

A good seafood supper for us now starts with a enough salmon for two, 2 cups of green beans, broccoli, or mixed vegetables, and 2 cups of grapefruit or pummelo pieces.

Put 1/4 cup olive oil in skillet with 2 garlic cloves finely chopped. Cook until the garlic is golden brown. Add the vegetables and stir fry 2 to 3 minutes or until they are crisp tender. Remove to a dish. Then fry the salmon until it is done (about 3 minutes on each side) and remove it to the top of the vegetables. Add about one cup of grapefruit juice, 3 Tablespoons of vinegar, herbs to taste and a dash of salt and boil until the juice cooks down to about half a cup.

Put the salmon in the center of a serving plate and drizzle some of the juice from the skillet over it. Add the vegetables to the skillet and mix until they are reheated and well covered. Then spread them around the salmon. Add grapefruit or pummelo sections and black olives (optional) around the edge of the plate and serve at once. This gives us enough salmon for two and vegetables enough for our daughter who doesn't like salmon.

I didn't think I would like pummelo mixed with the sauce, but found it quite good. So you can drizzle sauce on the pummelo pieces, too. This is an easy, quick, delicious dinner. If you like, add parslied potatoes on the side.

Betty Mackey's Baked Lemon Chicken

Take 6 boneless chicken breasts, cut them in half crosswise, and put them into a bowl. Add the juice of one large lemon and a tablespoon of vinegar or lemon vinegar (page 28) and/or one of grated lemon or orange zest (page 23). Add salt and black pepper to taste. Stir. Marinate for at least an hour, then arrange in a buttered baking pan. Top with bread crumbs and pour the remaining marinade over everything. Bake at 325 degrees F until cooked completely, about 40 minutes, basting once or twice. This dish will be very tender. Serve with salad and rice or potatoes.

Joan Blanco's Lime and Cucumber Salad

Slice 3 large young cucumbers into slices less than a quarter inch thick and put them in a mixing bowl. Add all the juice from one lime and a half a teaspoon of salt and toss. Place on serving plates and add salt and powdered cayenne pepper to taste. If you don't want so much heat, sprinkle the cucumbers with paprika instead for the color without all the fire.

Citrus Treats
Pieces of Citrus
Dip orange, grapefruit, or pummelo segments into your favorite yogurt for a satisfying and healthy snack.

Some people like to dip citrus sections in chocolate. I like to eat my chocolate and my fruit separately.

Add tangerine bits to coleslaw or tuna salad for a colorful, tasty surprise.

Add lime juice to salsa for authentic flavor.

Della Sarsfield's Kumquat Marmalade
-Cut kumquats in half, remove seeds, and chop.
-For every cup of chopped kumquat add 3/4 cup of white sugar and half a cup of orange juice or water unless they are very juicy. Mix well and let sit for an hour.
-Bring mixture to a boil in a stainless steal or other non-aluminum pan, reduce heat but keep the rolling boil and stir for about 10 minutes with a wooden spoon. If you don't keep stirring, it will stick.
-Put a little in a saucer and let it cool enough to taste. If it is not sweet enough for you, add a little more sugar and heat it some more. Stir well. Put the marmalade in jars, and when cool, refrigerate them.

Della says two cups of fruit is ideal and she wouldn't try to cook more than 4 cups at a time. She prefers the Nagami or sour kumquats, but I used my Meiwas and didn't need to add any more sugar.

After I made the above, I used the same pan to make the following:

Sugarless Kumquat Marmalade
Halve, seed, and chop fruit as above. For each pint of kumquats, add a pint of water and have on hand one small box of sugarless gelatin dessert about a third of an ounce – the .3 or .44 ounce size. Bring the fruit and water to a boil and then turn it back to medium.

Cook about 5 minutes until the kumquat pieces are tender. Stir occasionally, but it is not necessary to stir constantly since there is no sugar to make it stick. Then add gelatin powder and stir until dissolved. Remove from heat and when cool pour into jars. Refrigerate or freeze, but if you freeze, be sure to thaw it in the refrigerator, not at room temperature or it will separate. This is very low in calories, about 3 to a tablespoon, and tastes very good.

Citrus Blossom Tea

Like most other floral herbal teas, citrus blossom teas are made by collecting and gently washing the flowers. Use them at once or dry them for later use. Use one to two teaspoons of dried flowers or twice that amount of fresh ones for every cup of water.

To make the tea, steep the fresh or dried flowers in hot water which is at or almost at the boiling point until the tea reaches the desired strength. If you want the purest possible flavor, use distilled, filtered, or spring water. If your tap water is good you can use it and I often do. A ceramic teapot gives the best flavor.

You can make a pot full or make just one cup at a time. I sometimes use a jar, but not a metal container because metals might leach into the tea. You can put the citrus flowers into a tea ball or buy empty tea bags from a health food store. Fill these only halfway so the petals can expand as they steep. If you prefer, add the flowers directly to the hot water and later strain them out as you pour.

You can also add citrus flowers when you make sun tea or use them instead of regular or herbal tea bags. Place the needed amounts in a clear pitcher or jar to absorb the most rays and set this out in the sun for several hours to all day.

Once made, you can sweeten your citrus tea any way you would sweeten regular tea, but taste it first and then decide whether you want any sweetener or not. I doubt you will. Add lemon or lime if you want a slice of fruit. If the taste is too strong, dilute with as much water as needed.

You can also buy blends of citrus flower tea and follow the directions on the package.

Serve herbal teas hot or iced. Refrigerate any that is left over for up to three days. What is left can be frozen as ice cubes for flavoring drinks later or for cosmetics (see page 50).

28

Citrus Mint Punch
1 cup strong mint tea
1 cup orange juice
3/4 cup lemonade
1 cup crushed ice, plus more for serving
1 can (12 oz) ginger ale
5 slices of orange for the garnish
5 sprigs of mint for the garnish
5 citrus blossoms (optional) for the garnish
Combine the tea, orange juice, lemonade, and ginger ale with crushed ice in a pitcher. Pour into tall glasses over more crushed ice and add the garnishes. This makes five 8-ounce servings.

Easy Lemon Vinegar # 1
Combine 2 cups white vinegar or white wine with the rind of two lemons in a tightly covered glass bottle or jar and shake well. Set on a dry, cool shelf for ten days. Then you may strain the vinegar, replacing one piece of peel for identification if you wish. Mixed with olive oil this makes a delicious marinade or salad dressing.

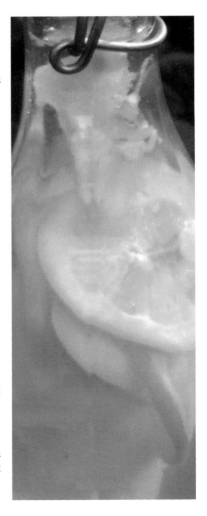

Easy Lemon Vinegar # 2
Slice about 2 lemons per pint and press them against the glass of a jar, filling in behind with other slices to hold the first ones in place. Fill the jar with white vinegar or wine and cover or cork. Treat as above. In an attractive bottle this makes a lovely decoration.

Easy Lemon Vinegar # 3
Pour 16 ounces of white vinegar into a stainless steel pan. Peel the zest from a clean lemon with a potato peeler and add it to the pan along with 2 bay leaves. Boil for 5 minutes. Cover and set aside until cool. Put in airtight bottle or jar and include the peel and bay leaves. Set on a shelf for 4 weeks. Then strain if you wish or use as it is. Let it sit longer if you want it to be stronger.

Candied Citrus Peel

My mother made this at least once a year, usually at Christmas time. When my sister first married and made it, her husband said, "I told her we didn't have to eat the garbage, but she insisted." It tastes good and looks pretty in the jar. It makes a good snack, also a garnish for meats, desserts, and fruit cups. Make some thinner strips and use them around the edge of a cake. Candied citrus peel can be cut up and used in fruit cake or cookies.

Mama's Grapefruit Peel Candy

Use peels from about four grapefruit. I made juice first, then scraped the thin white membrane and the rest of the pulp out. The thick white can stay.

Cut grapefruit peel into strips from 1/8 to 1/2 inch wide as you prefer and boil in small amount of water for 30 minutes, pour off, cover with fresh water and bring to the boil two more times. Modern recipes say boil for 5 to 20 minutes once and you can cut the peels before or after boiling. (I did one boiling for 30 minutes.) Drain off the water and use it on the garden or on houseplants after it has cooled.

Make syrup: 2 cups white sugar
1 cup water
¼ cup white Karo syrup
salt as needed

Put the peel back into the pan. Cook peel until most syrup is absorbed and peel is clear and almost transparent, 20 to 30 minutes, stirring occasionally.

Drain again, roll in sugar, and leave out to dry for two days. Then store in an airtight container.

This can be made with the peel of grapefruit, pummelo, or orange.

I did not much care for this as a child and still would not choose it over chocolate. At first it seemed to have a bitter after taste, but a light sprinkling with salt took that away. I now find a strip or two at bedtime is often satisfying enough to keep me from eating all the other things I might want to otherwise. It looks pretty in a candy jar and lasts a good while since it will not lead to overeating.

CITRUS AROUND THE HOUSE

Like other herbs, but perhaps more so, citrus lends itself to making household chores more simple and successful for less work, expense or exposure to more toxic material. It is a pleasant way to make better use of the resources we would often otherwise waste. If you take up the challenge, you may find, as I did, many happy surprises that make for better living with little or no cost or trouble.

Citrus for Fragrance

If you have an open fire, indoors or out, put oranges among the refreshments and throw some of the peels on the fire. Or save citrus peels just for this use. There is a high content of flammable oil in the skins and they make good fire starters or kindling. The fragrance of the orange oils will mix delightfully with the wood smell.

One of my friends, a vibrant young woman in her eighties, says her mother, who grew up right at the foot of the Alps in Northern Italy, used to tell how the ships would bring oranges from Sicily for St. Blaise Day (Feb. 2) and all the children would look forward to them. The hawkers would call out, "Two for a nickel, a dime a piece." And when the people were finished eating them, they'd put the rinds on the back of the stove and enjoy the fragrance all through the house.

Great Citrus Aromas and Air Fresheners

Fresh scent for closets. Dried citrus peels, especially of lemons, pummelos, and any orange with extra fragrance in the skins, can be used to add a pleasant mild scent to drawers or closets and reduce any musty smells. Cut the peel in small pieces and put in a cloth bag.

Repel flies and mosquitoes. A small pile of citrus zest will deter flies and mosquitoes from ruining your picnic or porch sitting without using any smelly poisons.

Perfume the car. Depending on the variety, whole citrus fruit gives out fragrance that has subtle changes in strength and aroma. I never quite appreciated this until I began hauling around baskets of pummelos to sell with my books. If I put them in the car the night before, the interior smelled wonderful for the ride.

Clean scent. The scent of lemon is synonymous with "clean" and is used in countless household products, soaps, perfumes, and cosmetics (see the next chapter).

Half a citrus fruit. Take notice of how half a lemon or orange in a dish can freshen a room. You can boil peels, after making juice or cutting up a single pummelo, to freshen the whole house. And grinding a few rinds in the garbage disposal will deodorize the drain.

Freshen the humidifier. Add a tablespoon of lemon or orange juice to freshen the aroma from your humidifier. Or use orange oil, details to follow.

Lemony dishes. A half a lemon in the dishwasher will result in sparkling, spot-free, clean smelling dishes and pots and pans. I was afraid there might be pulp left on the dishes, but there was not.

Air freshener. Make your own air freshener by mixing 1 cup of hot water with a tablespoon of baking soda in a small spray bottle. Then add a quarter of a cup of strained lemon juice. You can also use RealLemon for the juice (even if its date has expired). Shake well and spray. This will not have a long shelf life.

Remove odor. To remove moth ball odor from drawers or closets, wash the surfaces with a strong solution of lemon juice in water.

Remove fishy smells. Rub hands and cooking utensils with a cut lemon to remove fish smells.

Remove stains. Do the same to remove fruit and vegetables stains from hands.

Prevent cabbage odor. Put a lemon wedge in the pot when cooking cabbage to keep the odor from filling the whole house.

Potpourri

Citrus peels and leaves can add color and fragrance to potpourri and are also a fixative. For this purpose you can skin off pieces of the outside rind with a carrot peeler even before you eat the fruit.

Dry potpourri is a mix of fragrant, colorful dried leaves and flowers mixed with herbs, a few drops of essential oil, and a fixative such as orris root or citrus peels to help preserve the fragrance, sometimes for years.

Anyone who grows herbs can gather quite a quantity of the fragrant leaves over a few months by saving the leaves that must be stripped from the lower stems used for cuttings or for floral arrangements. Also save the petals of any unsprayed roses whenever you throw away a bouquet. These can simply be wrapped in a paper towel or placed in a paper bag and put on top of the refrigerator to dry them. Just add the pieces of citrus peel or citrus blossoms to this collection and let them dry. The paper bag is best because I have overloaded the top of the refrigerator on occasion and had herbs raining down. Or put them in paper bags and throw them in the back of the car for a

few days to dry out in the heat. Once these are dry, put them into airtight containers or zip-lock plastic freezer bags to preserve the most scent.

This combination alone is very fragrant and can be used for stuffing sachets made from small cloth bags (these can be very decorative) or tucked into empty tea bags that are available from health food stores.

Use the sachets in empty suitcases, the pockets of warm coats during the months they are not used, and in drawers with lingerie, gloves, or sweaters. Add a ribbon and hang them on hangers in the closet. Herbs smell much better than moth balls and serve the same purpose plus pleasant fragrance. Tuck some behind books on shelves to protect them from insects.

Our great grandmothers put strewing herbs under the rugs they beat on the line every spring. Today we can put them under the doormat, fold them into the folding bed or couch that is seldom opened, or place them under the floor mats in a car that needs air freshening.

Basic Potpourri Recipe

My basic recipe for making proper potpourri calls for mixing together
-1 quart dried herb flowers and leaves.
-up to 3 tablespoons of spices such as cinnamon or cloves.
-1 to 3 tablespoons of fixative to which a few drops of essential oil may be added.

By varying the combinations you can come up with many different fragrances and eye-

pleasing textures and colors, even adding small seedpods or cones. It is best to keep these in a covered container and only open the lid when you most want the fragrance to pervade the room. Rubbing the mixture between your fingers will also stir up the fragrance.

You might display these in open bowls for special occasions, but if left uncovered they will lose their fragrance much sooner. Adding a few drops of essential oil will revive them as needed. There are various other recipes for potpourri mixes.

Citrus Potpourri Mix

-4 cups of dried leaves of bergamot, lemongrass, lemon basil, lemon balm, lemon thyme, lemon verbena or marigold flowers
-1 cup each of slivered citrus zest, cedar shavings, and whole cloves
-1 to 3 tablespoons sweet flag, angelica root pieces, patchouli, or orris root
-a few drops of oil of sweet orange, lemon, or citronella

Citrus flowers are the epitome of fragrance, strong enough to scent a whole neighborhood, but not so strong as to ever be offensive. My mother could not bear the scent of gardenias. The only scent that seems too strong to me is night blooming jasmine. When we first came to Florida, I could smell the orange blossoms almost everywhere during the blooming time, even when there was not a tree is sight. Since I once lost my sense of smell for 18 months, I have had great appreciation for the stirring beauty of fragrance, and orange blossoms rate at the top of my list, especially since they last from February into March. I notice fewer groves and trees among the housing developments than a decade ago. While the citrus trees are blooming, I find garden chores to do as close to my trees and as often as possible.

Citrus for Decoration

Besides this fragrance, their many shapes, sizes, colors, and textures make citrus fruits, flowers, and foliage ideal to use in floral arrangements alone or with other plant material. Our citrus might as well look lovely until we eat it, which it does even in a basket on the kitchen table where it is an open invitation to grab and enjoy.

Citrus for Household Cleaning

Lemons and limes work best for this, but other citrus will do almost as well. These are among the strongest of food acids and ward off household bacteria. While most fresh lemons and juices are too expensive and delicious to use this way, you can use the fruit that falls early or is partially bruised so you don't want to risk using it and ruining a batch of juice for drinking. I don't have a lemon tree, but have found one in my neighborhood. I would have gone to the door and asked if I could pick up the dropped fruit, but much of it falls along the road outside the fence so I just pick it up as needed. The following are also good ways to put lemon to use.

Copper and metal cleaner. I received two pans with copper bottoms as wedding gifts and soon gave up trying to keep them shining. Fifty years later (I'll do anything for book research) I took half a lemon dipped it in salt, and scrubbed the smaller pot. In no time at all it looked better than it had in years. I scrubbed between other chores while I fixed dinner. It didn't come quite as bright as new, but almost. You can see the difference between the one that had the lemon rub and

the other in the photo. This also works on brass, aluminum and stainless steel or you can make a paste of lemon juice and cream of tarter and scrub with that.

Enamel cleaner. If you have an enamel pan with stains on the inside, fill it 3/4 full of lemon or orange peel, cover the peel with water and bring to a boil. Boil for 15 to 20 minutes. Pour out the water and rinds and rinse. Then wash in soapy water. Or use the pan to make orange oil (see next page). But do not let orange oil stand in any enameled pan. It could eat through the enamel. Even the homemade grade is powerful. Empty the orange oil into glass or plastic containers and wash and rinse the pan well.

Faucet shiner. Rub lemon halves on your faucets to remove lime scale, soap residue, and hard water stains. I had to leave these on overnight to get some of the scale off, but it definitely helped. You can do the same right on the porcelain if needed.

Glass and surface cleaner. Put equal parts of strained lemon juice, vinegar, and water in a small spray bottle and use it for an all purpose cleaner on mirrors, windows, counter tops, and the easier stains on clothes. Between uses, keep it in the refrigerator.

Heavy duty stain lifter. For difficult stains such as rust and mildew on clothes, make a paste of the lemon juice and salt, rub it on the stain, and dry the cloth outdoors in the sun. Repeat as needed until the stain is gone, then wash in cold water. This will even whiten tennis shoes.

Ink remover. For ink spots apply ample lemon juice right away.

Detergent booster. Add up to 1/4 cup of strained lemon or orange juice to boost your detergents's power in a washing machine cycle. This will help brighten whites and remove stains and also add a pleasant fragrance. Add up to 2 tablespoons of juice to household cleaners.

Chewing gum remover. The mild acid in lemon or lime juice will disintegrate chewing gum on shoes, clothing, or in hair. It works very quickly. Be sure to rinse it away once it has worked so as not to bleach the hair or cloth.

Grater cleaner. To clean and sanitize your food grater and get rid of the food particles that get stuck in the holes, rub both sides with half a lemon. The residue will come off easily. If any resists, use an old toothbrush to finish the job. Then wash and rinse thoroughly.

Cutting board freshener. Get your cutting board clean by squeezing the juice from half a lemon, rubbing it in, and leaving it to soak for 20 minutes. Then rinse with water. This will kill germs and remove strong odors, even garlic and onion.

Floor cleaner. Where oranges are more plentiful than money for cleansers, people have used an orange half in each hand to scrub floors.

Machine oil remover. Mechanics have used oranges to remove grease and oil from machine parts and from their hands.

Citrus wood

Orange wood with its fine, straight grain, has been used down through the centuries for inlays on furniture and otherwise in cabinetry, so if you have a woodworker among your family or friends, they might be interested in the larger pieces of wood when you prune..

The wood is said to be easy to work. In Mexico, it is carved into chessmen, toys and other articles. The wood of the sour orange is whitish to pale-yellow, very hard and fine-grained, much like boxwood. In Cuba is it used for baseball bats.

Citrus Vinegar as a Household Cleanser

Citrus vinegar in the making

Fill a large glass jar with citrus peels, any kind, and cover with white vinegar. Seal with a plastic lid if possible and let this sit for four weeks, shaking it every so often. Then strain and use, diluting it with water in most cases (½ cup to a gallon). It will help whiten and clean clothes if used with your laundry detergent. It will also clean floors (use ½ to 1 cup per gallon of water), windows (use ½ cup to a quart of water in a spray bottle), appliances, counters, and is a good degreaser for stovetops, but test a small surface first before using it widely. This should keep without refrigeration.

To clean your oven, spray or pour the citrus vinegar full strength on burned or crusted areas and let sit for 2 hours. Then wipe with a rag or sponge that has been dampened with warm water. You may need to repeat this, but the fumes are much safer and less expensive than chemical cleaners.

Make Your Own Orange Oil

By far the most exciting thing I have learned in the writing of this book is how to make and use **orange oil**. Now I can't imagine living without it and wasting all those citrus rinds for so many years. No more.

Getting enough citrus peels. If you grow oranges and make juice, you will have plenty of orange peels but may never waste a single one again. If you buy and eat your citrus, you can still save the peels in a ziploc bag or airtight container in the refrigerator until you get enough to use. Or just chop a few peels in a spray bottle or small glass jar and cover with vinegar.

Orange oil in the making

You can even put citrus peels in the freezer, add more as you get them, and bring them out when you have enough. This will save you money, make your life much more pleasant, and make for greener living, with fewer strong chemicals that can't be as good for your health or that of the planet.

Extracting orange oil. Orange oil, indeed the oil of any citrus, has many beneficial uses in the home and garden. Commercial grades can be purchased. Lower strength oils can be easily made at home in any of the three following ways.

1. The next time you squeeze orange juice, cut up a pummelo, or otherwise use several fruits, don't throw away the peels. There are several ways to extract the oil from them. The easiest is to put them in water in a container that is either granite, ceramic, or stainless steel (not aluminum), cover, and let sit for several days. Then strain out the liquid, now called orange oil, and put it it in glass or plastic jars with a lid. Use at once or store in the refrigerator or freezer. It seems almost as effective after thawing.

2. I have adopted this second way. I put the peels, still containing the albedo and even a bit of pulp into a large non aluminum kettle. Use at least 2 ounces of peels to a gallon of water. I use whatever I have, often half a pan or more, and water enough to cover. Put a lid on the pan, bring the water to or almost to a boil, and then turn it down to simmer for several hours or even overnight. This works well in a Crockpot. Because this fragrance fills my house, my husband is glad to hear that it won't harm people or animals. Then cool, strain, and use or refrigerate. I was not putting seeds or pulp in with the peels until I learned of the good things in the seeds. Now it all goes in. When the kettle cools, I pour the liquid through a strainer or colander and put it in the refrigerator. After several batches or as the season comes to a close in the spring, I put plenty in the freezer, leaving space in its container for it to expand slightly. It, too, seems almost as effective after thawing.

3. The third way involves drying the peels. This can be done by putting them in a shallow layer in paper bags in a warm place. Drying them outdoors in the sunlight can destroy some of the oils in the skins. When the peels are dry, grind them in a blender or food processor. Put the ground peels in a glass jar and cover with grain alcohol or vodka. Then put on a lid and set the jar or jars in a sunny place for several days. Shake them daily. After several days, strain the liquid through a coffee filter. Store it in a shallow dish with a cover, and when the alcohol evaporates, what is left is a fairly strong orange oil.

Orange oil ready to use.

Whichever method you have used, you strain out the liquid, now called orange oil, and put it in glass jars with a lid. This one may be strong enough to keep without refrigeration, but if you have room in the refrigerator, use it for maximum freshness preservation. Although it is strong, it is not pure oil the way an essential oil is.

After extraction, discard the peels in the compost pile or use them as mulch around almost any plants, but especially those than prefer acid soil. I don't think it will lower the pH level drastically, but the acid will be most welcome for azaleas, dogwoods, blueberries, gardenias, and camellias.

Whenever you grind peels in the blender, do small amounts at a time. Citrus peels are hard on the appliance. Mine has not died from the effort, but has sent out a warning, motor burning smell a few times.

Obviously, homemade orange oil will not have the strength of the commercial product and actually that is an advantage. Some commercial oils are strong enough to melt plastic. What I have made is not even sticky or in any way hurtful to skin, and because it is easy and inexpensive to make and keep on hand in large amounts, you can experiment with it.

Home Uses for Homemade Orange Oil

Fragrance. The orange oil has a pleasant fragrance that tends to uplift the spirit and calm the emotions. Add it when making soap, candles and other household products, or use it in a scent burner. Look at the Health and Beauty chapter (p. 45) for other uses.

De-greasing. Orange oil is a great de-greaser. Add some to your dish soaps or use it first instead. Commercial grades are used by one cruise line as a heavy duty de-greaser in the engine room. Citrus oil was even used to clean the oily rocks in Alaska after the Exxon Valdez oil spill. It is said to remove stains from garage floors and driveways but my homemade product was not concentrated enough to make much difference there. But it works very well on cleaning all of my pans and skillets, no matter how greasy, usually without any dish detergent. I just pour a little in, clean with a sponge, and rinse. It leaves just enough clean oil to keep the surface in prime condition. I also add it to my dish detergent in small bottles. Remember that orange oil has short shelf life.

You may well find it useful to clean stoves, oven, grills, floors, walls (it can remove crayon marks), and even tires and hubcaps.

I tried it on the car's windshield and my husband, until then a bit skeptical, decided it was a very good thing, especially during Florida's love bug season.

Stain removal and cleaning. I found that my homemade orange oil also removes stains from those dishes I put under plants for a time and then find them stained with rusty high water circles. Rub on the orange oil and let it sit for a while. This also works on dishes stained by blueberries or other foods and plastic containers greasy from the foods they have stored.

Orange oil is good for cleaning and revitalizing wood surfaces. It is often used in furniture polish. Orange oil is good for removing adhesives such as the stickers on glassware and other products when purchased. I use it to remove the labels on plastic containers. Orange oil will remove some stains from fabric, but it can stain light colors, so check its efficacy on a spot that won't show before you use it.

CITRUS IN THE GARDEN

Besides being beautiful, delicious, and productive, citrus is one of those plants that can make working in the garden more pleasant and productive by helping to control insects on plants and people, to ease sunburn, as a plant cleaner, and to encourage birds and desired wildlife. It also discourages cats from digging where you don't want them. When their indoor uses are exhausted, rinds can go into compost piles or worm farms. Read on!

Worm Bins at No Cost

A few worm bins by your compost pile will make the quickest, neatest compost you've ever had and the richest in worm castings. Citrus peels are fine for worms. There are worm bins available that can offer some special advantages such as worm tea. Check out the market if you are into high technology. But if you are into the simple and almost free, you need only a container with a few holes in the bottom big enough for a worm to crawl through. An old recycling bin or a large pot will do. Put it down on grass or soil (not cement) and then do not move it until the process is complete.

Cover the bottom with soil until none of the plastic or whatever shows. Old potting soil from plants past is okay for the soil layers. You can also use that extra soil along the driveway or the edge of beds, or take it from your paths as you lower them and effectively raise the surrounding area.

Then spread out a layer of edible vegetable material or leftovers from the refrigerator (even meat leftovers with a few bones are all right) coffee grounds with the filters, anything organic, including citrus rinds or what's left after making orange oil. I was very excited to learn that. No newspapers are used in this process and very few leaves. Cover all garbage layers with more soil, a layer thick enough so that you cannot see or smell or draw bugs to any of the garbage. The worms only work in the dark. Then continue to build this layer by layer, topping with soil. When the container is full, date it and wait three weeks or so while the worms do their work. The worm compost is ready to use in worm compost tea (plants love it) or soil amendments for your garden. It will make your plants thrive.

No, you don't have to add worms. Put out their food and they will come. You can put screening on top to discourage varmints, but nothing airtight. Water as needed in dry times but don't let the bin get wet enough to drown the worms.

When the worms are finished they leave that container for your next one. In winter they go wherever worms go in the winter, but in cold climates you could bring the bin into the basement or garage and have worms eating your kitchen scraps all year round. Be sure to put them outside again in the spring.

Worms from my worm bin

Citrus Oil Pesticides

Dana Venrick, Volusia County, Florida, Extension agent, says, "Citrus oil [the main active ingredient is D-limonene which is a component of Oroboost organic pesticide] has many beneficial uses in agriculture and home gardens as a pesticide. One of the best herbicides I have seen is used extensively by organic growers and is a combination of orange oil and commercial grade vinegar. D-limonene is also used in organic herbicide formulations. Orange oil kills termites and roaches on contact."

Dennis Gretton of D and D Growers in Lithia, Florida, grows herbs and sells most of them at plant festivals. "I was at one festival when the plant inspector came around and spent quite a while looking over my plants," he says. "Then he went on to inspect others. Later in the day he came back and asked what I was using as a pesticide. Our nursery is 100 percent free of poisonous pesticides, but I do use Oroboost (certified organic) right in the irrigation water." The inspector said that Dennis's plants were clearly superior to most of the rest he had seen that day.

I am glad to know that orange oil can work as a systemic pesticide, taken up by the roots to repel insects from the leaves. Now if I have any left over I pour it throughout the garden around the plants that I feel need it most, like the roses. The fumes or even full contact will not hurt people or animals, though cats don't like it.

But since it is an insect eliminator, do not use it except where it is needed because it could also kill bees, butterflies and many other beneficial insects.

Citrus oil kills insects by destroying the waxy coating on their exoskeleton so that they die from dehydration and asphyxiation. Especially since homemade oil is less strong than the commercially made type, you can spray orange oil directly on an insect-infested plant.

We don't have many flies in Florida, but I am excited to find that orange oil is effective as a fly spray because we had hundreds of them on our acreage in Iowa. Had I known, I would have imported citrus rinds by the truckload to spray the oil in the dairy barn. To think we always got a bushel of oranges for Christmas and I just threw the rinds in with the compost! The best part would have been replacing those toxic fumes from the fly sprays we did use.

Dog shampoo. Add some orange oil to your dog's shampoo to help with flea and tick removal. Or just rub it on the dog's coat after the last rinse. This will kill any fleas that have survived the bath and act as a repellent for those he might find in the grass at least for a short time. Using what you once threw away can save you a good bit of money. Do not use this on cats because citrus is toxic to cats in concentrated amounts.

Fire ants. Citrus oil, alone or mixed with molasses, repels and kills fire ants and similar pests. Mix 1 to 2 cups per gallon of soapy water.

Fruit tree spray. Citrus oil and molasses can be used instead of horticultural oil for spraying fruit trees.

Plant cleaner. Orange oil can also be used to clean plant leaves of dirt, mildew, or other buildups. The acid in the orange oil can also help destroy some bacteria or fungi. Use an ounce to a cup of orange oil, depending on the strength, to a gallon of water, and apply this to the leaves in the cooler part of the day (not when the sun is full strength on the leaves). If necessary and practical, rub away the soil with a soft rag.

Insecticide. Soak the following items in water overnight: orange and/or lemon peel, lavender leaves, mint leaves. By morning the water will have absorbed much of the oil from the herbs. Strain the solids out and put them on the compost pile. Use this water alone or with witch hazel as a natural insecticide around your home and in play areas where the children are often in the grass. It is safe for children and pets and will not hurt the skin.

With compost tea. Manure or compost tea is an effective killer of many plant pests because of certain beneficial microorganisms that exist in it naturally. One friend sent me a fancy box of tea bags with instructions to read the label carefully. Those bags containing manure are one of my favorite jokes. In college we learned to put manure in a bucket or barrel, add water, let it set for several days, and dilute to the strength of weak tea. I keep one of my rain barrels for this and do not add gold fish as I do to the others, but I have found some tadpoles in there. There is little if any smell.

Besides watering it onto the leaves and ground around any plants except those you plan to eat soon, you can strain this through old panty hose, cheese cloth, or frost cloth and use it as a foliar feeding. I have only recently learned that it is efficacious against insects and fungal diseases, especially black spot on roses and early blight on tomatoes. Add 2 tablespoons of molasses to each gallon of spray and add orange oil, up to a cup per gallon, for even more pesticide power.

For sunburn. I don't usually suffer from sunburn because I am outside in my garden so much. I wasn't worried when I had to sit in full sun for more than four hours selling books at a plant festival. It was only April and I had on a wide brimmed hat. That night my arms and hands were very red. I treated them with aloe from the garden, then later sloshed on some orange oil. By then I had a few gallons on hand. It took the burn right away. Later, there was none of the itching that usually comes as sunburn heals. I applied it again a few times, especially when I was going out in the garden. Guess what else I discovered:

Orange oil is a mosquito repellent! Mosquitoes have always loved my blood and have kept me out of the garden in the evenings for years. No more. I have had hardly a single mosquito bite since using the orange oil. If I forget to put it on or miss a spot, I still get some bites. In that case, I put the orange oil on the bites. It takes the itch away, and the bites disappear by the next day. It feels just a bit sticky to your hand as you pat it on, but it dries quickly and then doesn't feel at all sticky or unpleasant on the skin. When summer heat and rains came, it did not work quite as well, perhaps because by then I was using frozen orange oil, but more likely because we just have more mosquitoes in our rainy summers. But even then, I still got more evening time in the garden. If it works 99 percent for the citrus season and 50 percent for summer, I still consider it a Godsend.

Lemonade for plants. Lemonade applied to potted plants keeps their flowers fresh longer than normal. But it cannot be used on chrysanthemums without turning their leaves brown.

Uses for Citrus Fruit that Drops to the Ground

To feed birds, butterflies, squirrels and other wildlife, cut fruits in half. Prepare the fence or board by hammering in expose nails to hold the fruit halves and you can add fruit to it. If you put this in front of a window you look out of often, you can enjoy watching the visitors.

Citrus halves set out for treats for the birds.

When you first go out to the garden early in the season, take one of those fallen fruits, cut it open and rub the fruit over bare skin to deter mosquitoes and gnats. It may feel a little sticky at first, but it is good for your skin and much better for your system than poison sprays. Once you start to harvest and make orange oil, use that. It works even better.

Fallen fruits can attract fruit rats and fruit flies as well as some disease spores, so rake them up as needed and either bury them in the compost or under the mulch around your acid-loving azaleas and camellias. I only have one tangerine tree that drops much fruit. The rest we use before it gets to that stage or immediately after it hits the ground.

Citrus and Butterflies

Besides planting it for its beauty, bounty and fragrance, plant citrus to attract butterflies. Lemon, key lime, tangerine, and sweet and sour oranges, provide larval food, especially for the giant swallowtail (the largest butterfly to grace my garden). Some butterfly gardens I've seen include wild lime (*Zanthoxylum fragara*) which is a citrus cousin with foliage that is lime scented when crushed. On the Atlantic coast from Merritt Island south through the Keys, another citrus cousin, sea torchwood (*Amyris elemifera*), is sometimes used to attract several Florida swallowtail butterflies.

Uses for Citrus Peels

Fire ants. Puree some peels in about three cups of warm water in your blender and slowly pour this into anthills to rid your garden of fire ants. I used all the skin from a large pummelo and probably a quart of water, filled a two-pound nut container with the slurry, took it to the church garden where there was an extensive colony that crossed the sidewalk, and poured it in. There were still a few ants a few days later so I repeated the treatment. That was about the time when I made my first orange oil and I took some of that for a final treatment that probably was not necessary. The ants are gone now.

We have not had fire ants in our yard for the last three years and I have not been sure why. For a time I thought it was because I had used a soil activator called Medina (available on the Internet). Vicki Parsons of Neem Tree Farms used this and found it also helped plants survive the cold better and she reported no more fire ants. Soon I had no fire ants either. But now I wonder if that is at least partly because of all those citrus peels I've spread as mulch. I have certainly used more of them than I have of the Medina, of which I've used less than a gallon on selected plants.

Cats. We have almost always had a cat in the garden and I've never worried about their personal habits. But if you want to discourage your cats, or your neighbors' cats from using certain areas of your garden as a litter box, mix citrus peels ground in your blender with coffee grounds and distribute it in areas where you want to repel cats. If necessary, put down a second batch and wet it down. Again, be aware that grinding citrus peel, even with plenty of water added in, is a rough job for a blender. Do small amounts at a time.

My cat has been known to jump down from the roof via my plant shelves and has knocked over a few pots. She has also been known to play with my succulents until they became mere pieces. Now that I know cats don't like citrus, I have put small amounts of the above mixture as a dollop of mulch with the succulents and in a pan on the shelf to discourage her. In the weeks since then she has been jumping the other direction.

Compost. Citrus peels are easily composted and their oils and resins offer no danger to the soil. The thicker the rinds, the richer they are in nitrogen. They are high in phosphorus and surpassed for potassium only by banana peels. Fallen fruits or culls are also useful as fertilizer though they are not as rich because they contain a great amount of water.

Livestock feed. Citrus pulp has about six percent protein and is a great feed supplement for cattle. Citrus peel is now turned into pellets. For many years one of the grandfathered-in farms in our neighborhood put out truckloads of citrus peel for a great variety of livestock including cattle, goats, and pigs. We saw how they enjoyed and thrived on that golden goodness. Alas, development finally took over that old farm.

CITRUS FOR HEALTH AND BEAUTY

Citrus is one of the best sources of Vitamin C, which mothers push when colds and flu threaten. Vitamin C is necessary for healing wounds and for building healthy bones, skin, tendons, and tissues. Recent medical research suggests that it may help prevent cancer.

Vitamin C doesn't last long in the body and needs to be constantly replenished. Deficiency can cause joint pains, shortness of breath, irritability, and susceptibility to infections. This, the Florida climate, and the other herbs I eat regularly may be why I have hardly any flu or colds in my later years while I had many when I was younger, living in colder, citrus-scarce climates. I have more joint pains, but not the kind that require replacement parts as many of my friends have had.

Oranges and their cousins are a great source of potassium and this keeps our muscles moving. Oranges and tangerines are high in Vitamin A, important for bone growth and night vision. Orange juice is a good source of folic acid that is so important for expectant mothers, and Vitamin B that reduces the occurrence of birth defects.

The water and fiber from citrus add bulk to the diet and thus curb appetite and overeating. Grapefruit juice is one of the best detoxifiers you can get. This may be the reason for the frequent grapefruit diet fads. I definitely find that a swig of grapefruit juice will often settle my food cravings. If you don't like the tangy tartness, add some honey, which is also good for you. I like to mix my grapefruit juice with some orange juice to sweeten it.

Citrus is an excellent and delicious preventative medicine. It was found to be a cure for scurvy when merchant ships began to carry citrus because of its ability to stay fresh for a long time. Sailors soon found that their liver spots went away, that bones and muscles did not ache, and that their teeth stopped falling out. In 1747 a Scottish surgeon, James Lind, carried out a

test giving some of the men cider, some vinegar, some saltwater, and some lemons and oranges. The citrus groups improved so quickly that there was no doubt that citrus was effective.

In 1876 the Merchant Shipping Act in Britain made it mandatory for sailors of the Navy to drink lime juice as part of their ration, thus giving them the nickname of Limeys.

Citrus and Your Health

Research has indicated that citrus species contain compounds called flavonoids, carotenoids and limonoides. The flavonoids show potential antioxidant, anti-cancer, antiviral and anti-inflammatory influences and may also lower cholesterol. Pink grapefruit has lycopene and beta-carotene which have been linked to the reduction of the risk of prostate and breast cancer.

The concentration of these compounds seems to vary with the variety and the harvest time, especially in grapefruit. These compounds are highest in the leaves and fruit at early stages of growth and ripening, and decrease after maturation except in the seeds, which show a higher concentration than do orange and lemon seeds. It also seems that pink and red grapefruit cultivars may have greater advantages because of these limonoids, and the seeded ones may be better than the seedless ones for our health.

Neither the author nor the publisher of this book advocates ever using citrus or any other herbs or home remedies when consultation with a doctor is indicated. We take no responsibility for any uses of citrus or its compounds or other home remedies reported here. You should use citrus and any other herbs cautiously, especially at first, trying a small amount and watching for any ill effects or allergies. If these appear, stop the use immediately. If not, you may increase their use to a moderate level.

Some of what I write here is from personal experience and some from what other people have told me of theirs. Citrus can make a pleasant difference in the little ailments of life.

Sore throat. My mother was not a plant person, but still honey and lemon juice was our first and often only medicine for sore throats and coughs. These had the advantages of being on hand and having a pleasant taste. The combination tends to coat the mouth and throat. Lemon juice with salt or ginger is another recommended cold remedy and the ginger would also soothe the stomach.

Dandruff. Some people claim that lemon juice helps control dandruff. Try working a tablespoon of lemon juice into your scalp before a shampoo. After the shampoo, apply a mix of 2 tablespoons of water and 2 of lemon juice. Repeat every other day until the dandruff disappears. But don't continue such treatments after they cease to be necessary. Lemons have some surprisingly strong components.

Cleaning teeth. Orange twigs were used in some countries as neem tree twigs were in India as a precursor of the toothbrush. You might keep that in mind for emergencies.

Whitening teeth. Rubbing your teeth with the juice or peel of citrus fruits is a natural way to whiten your teeth at home. I tried it and found I'd much rather sit around with orange peel strips, the white side against my teeth, than any other method I've tried. But I actually saw little change, and not being very patient, I stopped. Later I read that it is unwise to do this more than three times a week. The citrus acid could possibly lower the calcium content of the tooth or deteriorate the enamel. You might do this for two weeks perhaps twice a year as needed. And during that time, brush your teeth with a mix of baking soda and salt at a ration of 3:1.

The baking soda kills bacteria before it can lead to plaque. Also, it reduces the acids in the mouth. Baking soda contains peroxide that also helps to remove stains. There is no danger in swallowing a bit of baking soda. But this also is not recommended for long term use because it is quite abrasive and can cause damage to the tooth enamel and make the teeth extra sensitive and vulnerable to cavities.

Gingivitis. In Italy, lemonade is used to relieve gingivitis and inflammations of the tongue, but prolonged use can erode tooth enamel, some say, to the level of the gums.

Other uses. Unsweetened lemon juice is widely used as a laxative and a cold preventative. For heartburn relief, add a teaspoon of lemon juice to 4 ounces of water and drink it.

Health Uses for Orange Oil

As massage oil in aromatherapy. Use orange oil (see page 28 in the household chapter) for a massage oil to use in aromatherapy. It calms anxieties and releases tension and is refreshing and relaxing.

In the vaporizer for steam inhalation. Add strained orange oil to the vaporizer or steam inhaler liquid to soothe respiratory problems. Add some to the humidifier as well.

If you don't have a vaporizer, pick a time when you have 20 minutes to half an hour to spare and will not have to go outdoors for a few hours afterward. Boil a large bowl full of water in the microwave or tea kettle with two cups of orange oil. After it boils, add any other healing herbs you have on hand. Then take a large towel and sit in a comfortable place with the bowl in front of you, but not in your lap in case of spilling. Close your eyes and lower your head slowly into the steam. Drape the towel over your head to make a tent and stay in the steam, but open a corner when you need fresh air. This also works as a wonderful steam facial. It draws out impurities, increases circulation, and eliminates toxins. Stay in the steam for at least 10 to 15 minutes and then rinse your face in tepid and then cold water. The leftover scented water can be added to your bath, used as a hair rinse, or put on the compost pile.

For soaking feet. At last, relief from my athlete's foot! The quantity of citrus oil I now produce whenever I make orange or grapefruit juice, and a lifetime of fighting the itch and discomfort of athlete's foot prompted me to try soaking my foot in orange oil, which has fungicidal properties.

Oh, what relief it gives. I tried the orange oil remedy for the first time in the evening. That night I omitted the doctor's prescription that had given me very little help. In the middle of the night I woke up with an itchy foot, but I had left the pan of orange oil in the bathtub, and a quick immersion took away the itch. Since then, I have been soaking them as needed and have never had such happy feet. When I finish soaking, I put the orange oil back in the refrigerator in a covered container.

After perhaps eight soakings over a two week period I was able to go for months without any itching or pain. When it returned, as it always does, the citrus season was past, but I had a good supply of orange oil in the freezer. I thawed it out, but used it cold because it feels good. My sister heats up what I shared with her, at least to lukewarm, in the microwave. She has different and more serious foot problems and finds the orange oil soaking very soothing.

I would recommend an occasional soaking of any feet, troubled and tired or not, with homemade orange oil. It is not so concentrated. If you have a rash on a part of the body that does not fit into a pan, dampen a clean cloth with the orange oil right from the refrigerator and place it on the troubled area. Re-soak the cloth as needed. Orange oil is anti-inflammatory and is good for any minor rashes. Just don't get it near your eyes.

For comfort. When I ran out of bubble bath, I added a cup of orange oil to the bath water. It doesn't have quite the same ambiance, but it leaves the skin soft and the hair silky. Now when I put it on to go to the garden, I also put it all over my face, especially on the wrinkles. It probably won't reverse them, but it feels like it tightens the skin a bit and it keeps the mosquitoes away. Since we often have mosquitoes carrying diseases, this in itself is a major relief.

Citrus for Beauty

There are many ways to use citrus to improve one's appearance, and I use the word beauty in that sense. I gave up long ago any hope of becoming a beauty and have tried to concentrate on developing in myself and recognizing in others the much more important inner beauty. But there is no doubt that the use of citrus as a herb can enhance your outer self as well.

Lemons are the leaders in this endeavor. You can substitute other citrus for many of these recommendations, but for bleaching, lemons work best.

For nails. If you want to brighten your fingernails or toenails, soak them in lemon juice for ten minutes. Or simply rub the lemon wedge onto your nails. This will work even better if you follow with a solution of equal parts of warm water and vinegar, then rinse well. This can be especially helpful for those of us who work in the garden and are lucky to get our fingernails clean, let alone sparkling.

For hair rinse. When I was a teen and hair coloring was considered cheap instead of essential, we who had blond hair still tried the lemon juice rinse for natural brightening. Mix 1 part strained lemon juice with 3 parts water and apply it to your hair after rinsing out the shampoo. The highlights it adds will be subtle and natural looking, but more dramatic if you can also then dry your hair in the sun. My blondest daughter tried it for me, mostly to see if the lemon juice should be rinsed out or left in. We decided it is best left in and the hair dried in the sun. If any bits of pulp stay in the hair,they brush out easily, but do that outdoors, too. I would not try it on my own hair now because I cherish all the darker color I have left among the gray. Lemon juice is also good for oily hair. For dry hair make a tea of citrus zest.

Citrus blossom tea can also be used as a hair rinse to lighten hair and make it smell exciting. See page 28 for tea directions. Or add it to your bath. Use it for a cleanser, skin refresher, or for other cosmetic purposes.

To remove blackheads. You can buy scrubs and patches, but they are expensive and they don't always work. Try applying lemon juice to the blackheads after a thorough face washing each night at bedtime. Your pores will begin to shrink in a few days and the blackhead will be less noticeable. If they have already become pimples, apply lemon juice on the spot twice a day and the pimple will heal quickly.

To ease acne. The hormones that cause acne also cause more than normal shedding of skin cells and these block the pores. Exfoliates will correct this problem. Then it becomes important to apply antiseptics and antibacterials that help prevent infections in the pores. Because it is important to keep an acid environment in the skin, avoid soap, which is alkaline. Also avoid products that contain alcohol.

Alpha-hydroxyl acids occur naturally in citrus fruit. They augment the skin's exfoliating abilities and decrease the buildup of dead skin cells. They have been shown to improve acne. The easiest treatment is to wash with hot water. Then squeeze a fresh lemon and apply the juice to the face with a cotton ball. Soak it in the lemon juice often and let the juice dry on the face for ten minutes. Rinse your face well with cool water. The lemon juice should have a slight sting or mild burn. If it is too uncomfortable, dilute the juice with filtered water.

To remove stains. To remove food or garden stains from fingers and hands, cut a lemon or lime in half and stick your fingers into the flesh. Rub the fruit over any stains on the hands until all disappear. Then rinse with water and dry.

For scars, skin diseases, and age spots. People have reported great results with this. One lady had used microdermabrasion and laser to get rid of melasma that darkened the skin of her face. When her treatments did not help at all, she started using lemons with excellent results; she said, "I put lemon on my age spots and on spots on my face and it got rid of them. You have to use it a couple times a day and at night leave it on overnight. It doesn't dry out the face."

Another person reported having spent $400 on laser treatment that didn't work. She began to use lemon juice every night on her hands. "I'm 58 years old. After a few days my sun or age spots were gone. Now my hands have soft skin and no spots at all. I'm still using it."

I tried this on the age spots on my hand and arms and saw little difference, but I quit after a few days. I am too used to the spots to be dedicated to their removal.

Limes instead of lipstick? Limes were used by court ladies in France in the eighteenth century to redden their lips. They carried the fruit with them and bit into it as needed. We might remember that at the end of a meal where lemon or lime slices or sections are used a garnish. It is less obtrusive than bringing out your lipstick and mirror, as was the custom in my mother's time, and which always embarrassed me.

For fun. Children make orange-peel teeth and wedge them over their gums for Halloween.

Make Your Own Cosmetics

Citrus scented deodorizing body powder. Peel the zest from about six oranges, grapefruits or lemons and dry as instructed on page 22 (kitchen chapter). Then grind the strips in a coffee grinder several times or in a mortar and pestle until they reach the fine powder stage.

Add this to an equal amount of unscented talcum powder, cornstarch, baking soda, or arrowroot. Start with an ounce of citrus powder to an ounce of the other choice. Apply with a powder puff or cotton ball.

50

Other possible deodorizing ingredients may take more labor, but you can grind oven-dried clean eggshells, or herbs such as sandalwood, marigold or violet petals, or the roots of orris, calamus, or licorice and mix these 1 to 1 with the powdered citrus zest in the recipe just given.

For extra fragrance you can add a few drops of essential oil of lemon, tangerine, bergamot or neroli. Lavender and rose oil also combine well with citrus and have anti microbial properties of their own, so experiment.

Liquid deodorant. For a liquid deodorant you can use a base of 1/4 cup witch hazel, brandy or vodka and add 1 tablespoon of freshly grated zest and 1/4 cup of distilled water. You may also add a few drops of an essential oil as mentioned above. Steep this mixture for one day in a covered glass or ceramic container. Pour the strained mixture into a spray bottle or use a decorative jar and apply with a cotton ball.

Cologne. Gather, wash and dry: 1 cup fresh unsprayed flowers, which can be lavender, rose petals, citrus blossoms or jasmine blossoms or a mix of any or all.

Steep in 1 ounce ethyl alcohol in a tightly sealed glass container at room temperature. Shake well every day for a week. Strain and store in a dark glass bottle with a stoppered lid and little air space. Use and enjoy.

Floral water. This is easy to make and can be used in a refreshing herbal bath, as an after-shower splash, or in skin cleansers. The ones you buy are distilled and will last indefinitely. The ones you make should be kept in the refrigerator and used within two weeks, so make small amounts.

Basic Floral Water Recipe
This can include citrus zest and/or citrus flowers.
6 tablespoons of chopped fresh herbs of your choice or 3 tablespoons of crumbled dried ones.
1 ounce of fresh flower petals or half an ounce dried ones.
2 cups water.
Place all in an enamel pan. Bring to a boil, then cover, reduce the heat, and simmer for 30 minutes. Let cool, strain, bottle, and refrigerate.

Selecting Citrus
for Home or Garden

Natsumikan oranges at the Florida Citrus Arboretum in Winter Haven, Florida.

52

Citrus Varieties and How They Grow

Here in this section of the book I introduce you to the most popular and available of the types of citrus you can grow or buy and enjoy and indicate ripening time in different regions of the country.

Sweet Oranges (*Citrus sinensis*)

Sweet oranges are the world's most popular citrus fruit and are sometimes divided into the subgroups sweet (common) oranges, navel oranges, and blood oranges. Trees tend to form a globe shape and grow

from 12 to 16 feet tall depending on the rootstock, though they can reach 25 feet. For best production, place trees at least 16 feet apart. Once mature, the foliage is hardy down to around 26 F and the fruit to 27 F.

The term "sweet" can be misleading, since the fruits combine sugar and acid, the sugars forming during the heat of the day and the acids during the cool of the night. The taste is sweetest in regions or years when there is a wide fluctuation between day and

Juice oranges fresh from the tree! night temperature. Commercially the navel orange and its varieties are the most popular for eating out of hand and the Valencia and its varieties are used mostly for juice, partly because they ripen late and for a long time. Homeowners have a greater choice. Navels do best in California, but we enjoy them in Florida as well.

Cara Cara navels taste sweet and have low acid. Great for eating, they have dark reddish pulp and juice in Florida, pink pulp in California. They ripen from November through February in Florida, November through March in inland California, and have not been tested in other areas.

Hamlins are sweet, good for eating or juice, hardy, productive, low acid, and nearly seedless. These ripen from October through January in

53

Florida and Texas, November through January in the Gulf Coast and the Desert Southwest areas, and are not recommended for California.

Parson Browns are sweet with low acid, good for eating or juice. The small fruit is seedy. These are not recommended for areas other than Florida where they ripen from October through March.

Pineapple oranges are sweet and spicy, good for juice or eating. Trees are less hardy, alternate bearing, and tend to drop fruit when ripe. These ripen December through February in Florida and Texas, October through February in the desert (desert areas of California and Arizona where citrus is grown), and are not recommended for other areas.

Shamouti or Jaffas are sweet for eating and juice, have few seeds, heavy crops of large, thick skinned, delicious fruit. These ripen from December through March in Texas and are not recommended elsewhere, though we have some in Florida.

Valencias taste slightly acid and are good to eat. They are great juicers with few seeds and fruit that holds a long time on large, vigorous trees. There are several kinds. They ripen from March through June in Florida and Texas, February through May in the western desert, April through October in coastal California, and March through August in inland California.

Washington navels have excellent taste. They are the original and most widely grown navel oranges. They are easy to peel and hold well on the tree. They are best from November through January in Florida, Texas and the Gulf Coast, November through December in the desert, January through May in coastal California, and mid-November through April in inland California.

Blood Oranges *(Citrus sinensis)*

We use our blood oranges mostly in juice where they add excellent flavor, rich and berry like, and surprising color whether mixed with other varieties or alone. Ours start out with small flecks and get redder toward the end of the season. The pigments increase with cold weather. The name is not a marketing success and the Moro type can get quite purple, which some people don't appreciate. The juice looks like grape but tastes like orange. The color varies from place to place, year to year, and early winter to late winter. The best growing regions for them are the warm inland valleys of California, but they do fine in Florida, too. They are seldom seen in American markets, but are quite popular for

'Budd' blood orange

54

eating, juices, and garnishes in Europe. They have few seeds, but don't hold on the tree as long as regular sweet oranges.

Budds have a sweet, distinctive taste, are good for eating and juice, and have the deepest red pulp the soonest. They hold well on vigorous, very productive trees and ripen mid season. They are grown mostly in Florida.

Moros have a sweet/tart taste and are good for eating or juice. The color is more reliable in western states, the flavor good everywhere. The tree is vigorous but slower to bear. Harvest fruit from December to February in Florida, December through March in Texas and the Gulf Coast, February

through April in the desert, April through June in coastal California, and March through May in inland California.

Sanquinellis taste sweet and sprightly, good for eating and juice. The small oval fruit has a red blush on smooth skin. The tree is compact and productive. Pick from February through April in Florida, the Gulf Coast, Texas, and the desert, April through June in coastal California, and March through May in inland California.

Taroccos have a rich, berry taste, good for eating or juice. The tree is not as productive and can be thorny. The fruit is large with excellent flavor. Tarroccos are not recommended for the desert and are untested in the Gulf states. They ripen from March through May in coastal California and from January through March in inland California.

Sour Oranges *(Citrus aurantium)*

Sour oranges were and still are, to some extent, used as rootstocks. Although they are not as acidic, Florida natives assure me that the fruit and juice can do anything a lemon or lime can do, including making a pie according to any Key lime recipe. Use sour oranges for drinks, jams, chutney, sauces, candied fruit and marinades. The Chinese use both the flowers and the fruit for herbal teas and medicines. Commercially they are used for flavorings and liqueurs such as Grand Marnier and Cointreau and to make orange flower water, perfume, and orange rind oil. We made and enjoyed much sour orangeade. When my friend Betty came to visit, the sour oranges were the only ones she took home, for marmalade. The trees are easy to grow and cold hardy, but we never could use even half of ours and I needed the space so we took it out. Betty is still sorry. If you know someone who has one, they will be glad to share the fruit.

When we last visited the Florida Citrus Arboretum in orange blossom time, the most beautiful of the trees was a sour orange called 'Bouquet de Fleurs.' There was also a variegated sour orange 'Panache' with the leaves edged in white and green stripes on the bottom of the fruit. These can be grown in containers where they can be kept to six by six feet. They will bloom both spring and fall and bear fruit over much of the year.

This sour orange is variegated.

Mandarins, Tangors, and Tangelos (*Citrus reticulata, C. unshiu, C. deliciosa, and C. nobilis*)

This diverse group includes many hybrids. As a rule the mandarins are sweeter than the sweet oranges, with subtle blends of aromatic, sprightly, spicy and delicious flavors and aromas. Most have orange rinds and orange red juicy fruit that is easy to peel and separate into sections.

The trees can be tall and upright to almost weeping. The foliage is dense and the fruit visible on the outside of the canopy. Mandarins include tangerines but that is not a botanical term. It probably came about when most were grown in Morocco and shipped around the world from the port of Tangier. The foliage is hardier than that of sweet oranges, down to 24 F, but the fruit is slightly less hardy, down to 28 F. The trees can be alternate bearing, heavily laden one year, sparsely the next. The fruit does not stay long in prime condition and if left too long on the tree can become puffy and dry. By planting a selected few kinds, one can have these from November until June. Often the rind will tear away from the stem when picking, so shears or clippers are needed. The fruit varies from seedless to seedy, depending partly on variety and partly on isolation.

A **tangor** is a cross between a mandarin and a sweet orange, the most popular example being the temple orange.

A **tangelo** is a cross between a mandarin and a grapefruit or pummelo, and there are also some that have grapefruit or tangelo in their background and are thus labeled as tangelos.

These varied fruits are easy to peel and so delicious they are best eaten fresh, though I make juice out of almost any citrus. Some of these crosses appeared naturally, and some were created by plant breeders. The trees are smaller and less dense than most grapefruit trees and do best in warm summer climates. They will bear more fruit, but it will be seedier, if there is another mandarin or tangor nearby for cross-pollination.

56

Minneolas have rich taste and are the most popular for eating or juice. They are tart in colder climates or before they mature. They have a neck and hold well on large, attractive, hardy trees. They are at their peak from December through February in Florida and Texas, from January through March in Gulf areas and inland California, from January through February in the western desert, from March through May in northern coastal California and February through April in southern coastal California.

Honey Murcotts have a sweet, rich taste and are great for eating or juicing. They are easy to peel. They hold very well on trees that bear heavily in alternate years and may need support. Their parentage is unknown. Harvest honey murcotts from January through March in Florida, Texas, and inland CA, from March through May in coastal California. They are not recommended for other areas.

Orlando tangelos taste sweet and mandarin-like and are good to eat or juice. The medium to large fruit grows best in warm climates and holds well on large, hardy trees. A pollinator increases production. Pick ripe fruit from

November through January in Florida and Texas, December through February in Gulf Coast and inland California, and November through December in the desert. Orlandos are not recommend for coastal California.

Wekiwa tangelos are mildly sweet to eat or juice. The fruit is pink in warm climates, more like a small grapefruit. These ripen from November through January in Florida. Elsewhere, check with local agricultural extension offices for specifics.

Mandarin oranges are diverse

Temples taste rich and spicy and are great for juice and eating fresh. This type is probably from an orange crossed with a pummelo. The small to medium fruit holds well on spreading trees with many thorns. They ripen from January through March in the Gulf states, January through February in the desert, and February through March in inland California. They are not

WEKEIWA TANGELO

recommended for coastal California areas.

Orantiques taste sweet to eat or as juice. The fruit is medium in size, is slightly flattened, and has a small navel and few to many seeds. These ripen from March through June in Florida and April through late May in the San Joaquin Valley in California.

Clementines have a sweet, apricot like taste, are good for eating or juice, and are easy to peel. This decorative weeping tree bears well in containers. There are several hybrids. Pick ripe fruit from November through January in Gulf areas, the Southwestern desert, and inland California, from January through mid-April in coastal California.

Dancy Tangerines have a good, sprightly taste for eating or juice. The abundant fruit has dark orange pulp and is a traditional Christmas treat. It ripens from December through January in Florida and the desert, December through February in Texas and the Gulf Coast, February through mid-April in coastal California, and January through March inland in California.

Honey Tangerines are sweet to eat or juice, hold well on the tree, and are easy to peel. The fruit is small but the tree large and highly productive. It is not recommended for the Gulf states. It ripens December through February in the desert, February through April in coastal California, and January through March in inland California.

Page oranges have an excellent, rich flavor to eat or juice. The small fruit is very ornamental on a large tree. It is a Clementine mandarin-Minneola tangelo cross. Harvest fruit from November through January in Florida, January through March on the Gulf Coast, December through February in Texas, February through May in coastal California, and December through February inland. It is not recommended for the desert.

Ponkans, my favorites, have excellent sweet flesh for eating fresh. The large fruits are too good to use for juice. They are easy to peel. The skins nearly fall off when mature. The

Honey Tangerines

branches should be pruned rather short after harvest or the fruit will weigh them down. Before harvest they may need some staking. They are best from December through January in Florida, the Gulf Coast, and Texas and are not recommended for other western areas.

Satsumas taste sweet and sprightly to eat or juice. There are several hybrids. Satsumas have few seeds, and trees are slow growing but spreading. They ripen from October through November in Florida and

Texas, November through December in other Gulf states and in inland California, from December through April in coastal California, and are not recommended for the desert.

Grapefruit *(Citrus paradisi)*

Grapefruit gets its name from the young flowers hanging in bunches. It is considered a mutation of the pummelo and was first seen in the eighteenth century. The flavor is a sweet-tart that is quite delicious alone or with sugar, honey, or syrup added. It is extremely nutritious, with one half providing half of a daily dose of vitamin C. But it contains a chemical that may interfere with the absorption of certain medicines. It also appears that the red flesh is more nutritious than the white.

The fruit needs hot summers for best taste and the flesh can be white, pink, or red, all of which need heat rather than cold to develop. Unlike oranges, the color does not affect the taste. Fruit is good fresh, in salads, as juice, canned or frozen as juice-covered segments, in jam, or as candied

peel. It can ripen in as little as six months or take as long as a year or longer, in which case the tree will bear overlapping crops. Longer ripening means a greater chance of cold damage. The trees are ornamental and if not pruned back they grow very large and should be spaced 14 to 16 feet apart.

Duncan has superior flavor for eating or juicing. This old variety is still cherished, though the fruit is seedy. The pulp is yellow, the fruit large, and the

DUNCAN GRAPEFRUIT

tree productive. Duncans ripen from November through May in all areas except for California, where this variety is not recommended.

Marsh has fine flavor for eating or juicing and is most desired as it is almost seedless. It has white flesh and holds for a long time on large, vigorous, spreading trees. The fruit ripens from November through May in Florida and Texas, December through May in other Gulf states, January through May in the desert, April through August in northern coastal California, April through November in southern coastal California, and from February through August in inland California.

Red Flame has fine flavor for eating and juicing. It is widely planted in Florida for its deep red pulp, red blush on the rind, and few to no seeds. It ripens in January and February in Florida, from December through February in the western desert, March through May in San Joaquin, and May through October or whenever they fall in Southern California. Check with your Extension Office for local ripening times in Florida.

Rio Red has excellent flavor for eating and juicing. The large fruit is similar to Red Flame, nearly seedless, and holds well on large, vigorous, reliable trees. Rio reds ripen from December through May in Florida and Texas, from November through May in Gulf states, from December through April in the desert, from January through May in inland California, and from April through November in coastal California.

Star Ruby has fine flavor for eating or juicing and the reddest colors so far. Its quality is excellent. The fruit is small with less acid and few to no seeds.

Rio Red grapefruit

It holds well on the trees, but the trees are small, sparse, and slow growing. Fruits ripen from December through May in all Gulf states, December through April in the desert, January through May in inland California, and April through September in coastal California.

Pummelos *(Citrus grandis, C. maxima)*

Pummelos are the granddaddy of the grapefruit and the largest by far of any citrus with fruits that can reach four pounds apiece. This is one of the few citrus that will come true from seed (Key lime is another), but it can take 15 years or more to start bearing. The fruit is drier and less acid than grapefruit. It is usually eaten after separating the sections and removing the strong membranes. Sometimes the pieces are used in salad. It seldom needs any sweetening. For best flavor, let pummelos sit for a week or two after picking them. Segments set out in a dish with toothpicks make a delightful snack. I

seldom try to juice them but some people do. The thick rind can be candied and has a distinctive taste.

Pummelo trees are native to Southeast Asia and people from that part of the world are very fond of them. The trees require hot summers. My tree,

almost 20 years old, is only a bit larger than my orange trees and is much more reliable and productive than my grapefruits. Pummelos are a little hardier than grapefruits. The heavy fruit hangs mostly to the inside and lower part of the tree. It seldom drops and the load has never broken a branch. I get about 70 large fruits in partial shade. My

RFCI friends get up to 200 from one tree in the sun. There are several varieties and hybrids. I've tasted widely and still prefer my Hirado Buntan, though the Sha Tian You that I tasted was almost as sweet as candy.

They are sometimes called shaddock after the captain of an East Indian ship that brought seeds to Barbados around 1700. They vary in size, shape, and color of pulp. Here are some of the popular pummelos.

Chandler tastes sweet to eat out of hand or in salads. It is bell shaped, very large, borne in clusters with pink flesh on medium to large tree, widely grown in California. It ripens from November through February in Florida and Texas, December through February in the desert, December through April in inland California, and April to June in coastal California.

Three large pummelos with a grapefruit

Chuiyuk is small and chewy for eating and salads. The oval fruit has green skin with white chewy flesh.

Hirado Buntan (Butan) is very sweet for eating plain or in salads. It has large, rounded, slightly flattened fruits with pink flesh, and is a Florida favorite where it ripens from November through May. It is rare in California.

Liang PinYau is sweet with large, oval shaped fruit, thick flavedo, and pink flesh with many seeds. It is highly favored in Asia for desserts.

Siamese Pink and **Sha Tian You** are also large sweet pummelos that grow in Florida and ripen from November through May.

Pummelo x Grapefruit Hybrids

These crosses between pummelo and grapefruit are mostly grown in western USA states.

Melogold is delicious for eating, tastes more like pummelo, ripens later, and is a bit sweeter than Oroblanco but less cold hardy. It ripens from December through January in the desert and inland California, and from February through April in coastal California.

Oroblanco is sweet, good for eating or juicing, and slightly larger than grapefruit. It is often borne in clusters on a handsome tree. The rind is still partly green at peak

ripeness. Harvest this one from November through January in the desert and in inland California, from January through April in coastal California.

Lemons *(Citrus limon)*

Lemons are valued not so much for what they are but for what they do. They have the most herbal uses of any citrus. Every household should have access to a lemon tree. The bright yellow fruit enhances flavors, turns ordinary dishes into something special, and serves as a salt substitute. Lemon-

Sanbokan is a very sweet lemon

ade is synonymous with refreshing coolness on a hot summer day. Lemon, even the fragrance, means clean in household products and cosmetics.

True lemons such as Eureka and Lisbon are found in the supermarkets. The Improved Meyer is probably a hybrid between a mandarin or an orange and a lemon. The first two do best in California. The Meyer is the better choice for Florida and it is also hardier.

Lemons will bear fruit in cooler climates and are ideal for container plants. In the garden they are very vigorous and bloom and can be harvested throughout much of the year. They require some pruning to keep them neat and new growth and flowers are often tinged with pink or purple. If pruned they can be planted every 12 feet and form a hedge. They can also be espaliered on a trellis or against a wall.

Lisbon, the preferred supermarket lemon, tastes tart and acidic and is hardier and more heat tolerant than Eureka. It holds well on vigorous, dense trees that need regular pruning. It is not recommended for Florida and the Gulf states, but ripens from August to March in Texas, September to January in the desert, October to June in inland California, and year round in coastal California, so they are always available in grocery stores.

Eureka is tart and strongly acid, good for juice and herbal uses, medium in size with a tight yellow rind and few seeds. It is hard to peel, and holds well on a

Eureka lemon

63

vigorous open tree that is smaller and has fewer thorns than Lisbon. It is not recommended for Florida or the Gulf Coast. It ripens from August through March in Texas, September through January in the desert, October through June in inland California, and all year in coastal California. **Variegated Pink Eureka** is very ornamental with its green and white striped leaves, but it is harder to grow because the white part of the leaves does not make chlorophyll. The young fruit is also variegated, with the striped rind fading to yellow. It is small and is often ribbed. The flesh is light pink.

Meyer has a flowery, tart taste, great for juice and herbal uses. It is hard to peel. Medium in size, it has a thin rind and dark yellow flesh. It holds well on small, spreading, hardy and productive trees with few thorns. It ripens from November through March in all areas except coastal California where it is harvested year round and is the lemon of choice.

The **Ponderosa** lemon has a tart, acidic taste and is good for juice and herbal uses. It is a lemon-citron hybrid. Its fruits are huge and bumpy, with a very thick rind and many seeds. It holds well on trees that are only half the size of the true lemon. They are also thorny and less hardy than other lemons. They ripen year round in all areas.

Sanbokan is a sweet lemon that is great for juice or eating fresh. It is a Mandarin orange x lemon cross and tastes like biting into a glass of sweetened lemonade. The fruits are pear shaped and have knobby rinds with delicious pulp. The upright trees are self fertile and cold hardy. The fruit ripens from January through March in inland California.

Limes *(Citrus latifolia, C. aurantifolia)*

Limes come in small fruited and large fruited varieties. They will turn yellow if left on the tree, but commercially are picked green to avoid confusing customers. When not in fruit, lime trees differ from lemons in that they have wider petioles or leaf stems. The taste of the lime has a distinctive tang and the color does not indicate ripeness. Juiciness does. Both kinds are more susceptible to freeze damage, but the small ones especially so. Limes tend to do better in Florida and other warm summer areas than do lemons.

The small Key limes are most cold tender and grow on twiggy trees with open habit. The Persian limes grow on ornamental trees that are handsome in the landscape or in containers. All are used in cooking, baking, limeades, and mixed drinks. They have many herbal uses.

Bearss has excellent flavor for juice. Its fruit is larger than Persian, the tree is larger and more erect. It is the most common commercial lime, smaller than lemons and slightly hardier. The fruit is green, then yellow, with few seeds. The trees are small and compact. It is the best lime for containers because it is the least thorny. These limes ripen all year in Gulf Coast states, August through January in the western desert, August through March in northern coastal California, from August through May in southern coastal and inland California.

Key Lime ripens all year

Key Lime has excellent flavor for juice or Florida's famous pie (page 25). It is the most frost sensitive of citrus, with small round or oval fruit which is very aromatic and juicy. It does not hold well on the tree after the fruit starts to yellow. The tree is small and thorny. This one ripens year round in all areas.

Kumquats and Hybrids *(Fortunella crassifolia, F. margarita)*

Kumquats are the smallest of citrus and unique in their botanical name and the fact that you eat them rind and all, and just spit out the seeds. The fruit is cold sensitive, but the small, ornamental trees are among the hardiest of the citrus. They get about 12 feet tall in the ground, but stay smaller in containers. They don't bloom until midsummer and stop growing earlier in the fall.

Because kumquats are so hardy, they are used to breed other cold-hardy citrus. Kumquat hybrids such as limequats are good substitutes for lemons and limes.

The **Meiwa kumquat** is delicious right off the tree, though some people prefer the tart **Nagami**. Either is good sliced in salads or stir fries, candied, pickled, baked in breads, pies, jams and chutney. They make a great sauce for meats.

Our Meiwa is the only citrus tree we have from which we can't use all the fruit, but many of our friends are glad to help. The size of the fruit varies from year to year and gets largest when there is plenty of rain between blossom and fruit set.

Meiwa has a sweet, tangy taste and is good for eating or cooking. Fruit is small, round, and very tasty eaten whole, skin and all, or in jams, candied, pickled, or in sauces. Trees stay small and attractive, are good in containers or landscapes. They ripen from November through March in Florida and Texas, December through March in Gulf Coast states, desert states, and inland California, and January through March in coastal California.

Nagami kumquats taste tart and tangy and are good for eating or cooking. Fruits are small but elongated with only one to three seeds. They have little juice but are good for jams. The trees are very attractive and fruitful. The fruit ripens from November through March in Florida and Texas, December through March along the Gulf Coast and inland California, from December through January in the desert, and January through April in coastal California.

Nagami Kumquat

Calamondins are sour but are great for jams and culinary uses. They are festive as houseplants in regions where citrus is not hardy. There are masses of flowers followed by small round orange fruits. Calamondins may be a cross between mandarins and kumquats. There is a variegated form. The fruits ripen and turn orange from October through January in Florida, and year round in inland California. They vary in other areas.

The **Tavares limequat** is an excellent substitute for lime and much hardier. It is a cross between a Key lime and a Nagami kumquat, with larger fruit which is light green to orange-yellow. Fruits are juicy with few seeds,

66

hold well on compact trees, and are very ornamental and productive. These ripen from November through March in Florida and Texas, from December through April in the Gulf Coast, and from December through July in coastal California. Fruiting time varies in other areas.

The **Eustis limequat** is lime like, tropical, and good eaten whole. The fruit is a small oval and turns from greenish to yellow if fully ripe. Fruits hang for a long time on small, open trees. Eustis limequat is hardier than limes but less so than kumquats. Pick ripe fruits from November through March in Florida and Texas, December through April in the Gulf Coast, November through April in western desert states, November through May in inland California, and December through July in coastal California.

The **Lakeland Limequat** is similar to Eustis in all ways but is larger and more orange in color.

For Further Information

There are countless types and species of citrus, so always be open to tasting new kinds. If you are selecting trees, go to Rare Fruit Council International meetings and its citrus tasting events. Visit citrus arboretums near home and when you travel. Talk to other growers and nursery people and get their best advice. Learn from your citrus growing friends and from Master Gardeners and enjoy the adventure as you do so.

Monica Brandies, Author

Monica Moran Brandies lives near Tampa and grows herbs, fruits, vegetables, and ornamentals in her half acre yard. She has been writing about her garden adventures since college days at the Pennsylvania School of Horticulture, now part of Temple University. She was awarded the title of Alumni Fellow after giving a talk there in 2008. Her articles and photos appear in the *Brandon News Weekly* and in most issues of *Florida Gardening Magazine.*

This is her third book on herbs but her work covers other garden topics. Her popular books include *Ortho's Guide to Herbs* (Ortho Books); *Herbs and Spices for Florida Gardens*, *Florida Gardening: The Newcomer's Survival Manual*, and as coauthor with Betty Mackey, *A Cutting Garden for Florida*, all from B.B. Mackey Books (**www.mackeybooks.com**), as is her one non-garden book, *Bless You for The Gifts.* Her other books include *Xeriscaping for Florida Gardens* and *Shade Gardens for Florida* (Great Outdoors Publishing, now part of Finney Co.), and Sunset's *Landscaping with Tropical Plants.* She coauthored *The Florida Gardener's Book of Lists* (Taylor Publishing) with Lois Chaplin, and she is one of several contributors to an organic garden tips book from Rodale Press.

She originally started gardening to grow food for her family and managed to grow about 90% when she was feeding their family of nine children. In her garden and in her writing, she now specializes in attractive and useful plants for Florida gardens including citrus, herbs, fruit trees, vegetables, and decorative plants. She is a longtime member of the Rare Fruit Council International. She and her husband David are now semi retired and enjoying it greatly.

For links to more information about Florida gardens, copies of many of her garden columns, and color photos of many plants and gardens, visit her web site, **www.gardensflorida.com.** There you will also find Monica's

schedule of events, the list of the topics she covers in her talks, and information on how to contact her about speaking to your organization or garden club.

Bibliography and Resources

Editors of Sunset Books. *Sunset Citrus.* Menlo Park, California: Sunset Publishing, 1996.
Florida Department of Citrus. *Florida Citrus Cookbook.* Atlanta: Marmac Publishing, 1985.
Maxwell, Lewis. Numerous titles. Tampa: Lewis Maxwell, Publisher
Page, Martin. *Growing Citrus: the Essential Gardener's Guide.* Portland: Timber Press, 2008.
Susser, Allen. *The Great Citrus Book.* Berkeley: Ten Speed Press, 1997.
Walheim, Lance. *Citrus: The Complete Guide.* Tucson: Ironwood Press, 1996.

Florida Gardening Magazine
Florida's Own Home Gardening Magazine
P. O. Box 500678
Malabar, FL 32950-0678
www.floridagardening.com

IFAS (Institute of Food and Agricultural Sciences)
www.ifas.ufl.edu/
IFAS publications (including Fruit Crop Fact Sheets and other publications of interest to home fruit tree growers) are available for free from their web site as well as from County Agricultural Extension offices.

ECHO's Edible Landscape Nursery
www.echonet.org/nursery.htm
Information related to ECHO's nursery
www.echonet.org/ ECHO website

UCR Database on citrus varieties
http://www.citrusvariety.ucr.edu/

Variegated Pink Eureka lemon

69

Index

CPSIA information can be obtained
at www.ICGtesting.com
Printed in the USA
243691LV00001B

9781893443181